NEIL KINNOCK

MAKING OUR WAY

Investing in Britain's Future

Basil Blackwell

Copyright © Neil Kinnock 1986

First published 1986
First published in USA 1987

Basil Blackwell Ltd
108 Cowley Road, Oxford, OX4 1JF, UK

Basil Blackwell Inc.
432 Park Avenue South, Suite 1503
New York, NY 10016, USA

British Library Cataloguing in Publication Data
Kinnock, Neil
  Making our way: investing in Britain's
  future.
  1. Great Britain – Industries
  I. Title
  338.4'767'0941   HC256.6
  ISBN 0–631–15384–5
  ISBN 0–631–15385–3 Pbk

Library of Congress Cataloging in Publication Data
Kinnock, Neil Gordon, 1942–
  Making our way.
  Includes index.
  1. Public investments – Great Britain. 2. Great
Britain—Economic policy—1945–   . I. Title.
HC260.P8K56   1986   338.941   86–17582
ISBN 0–631–15384–5
ISBN 0–631–15385–3 (pbk.)

Typeset in 11 on 13pt Plantin
by Joshua Associates Ltd, Oxford.
Printed in Great Britain by Billing and Sons Ltd, Worcester

Contents

to
Glenys,
Rachel and Steve,
who give me joy

Preface

Socialists are made in many ways. Some are socialists because of their own experience of poverty or other forms of oppression. Some are socialists out of pity for the plight of others. Some are made socialists by the injustice of the privilege system, others by the gross inefficiency of its production and the rapacity of its exploitation.

Some are socialists because of opposition to aggression, others are socialists because they have to fight for their lives. Some socialists take all of their socialism from internationalism, most socialists owe something of their socialism to that and also relate their thinking and action to the differing realities of their countries and continents. There are cerebral socialists and cardiac socialists and gut socialists and doubtlessly too, there are socialists who, as George Orwell complained, have a 'hypertrophied sense of order'.

There is, in short, no neat package of philosophy or people of socialism. Socialists have to speak for themselves and, if they are democratic socialists, they will be doing their best to ensure that others get and keep the freedom to speak for themselves too. Indeed, they will not confine themselves to that ambition. They will be seeking the freedom for all to express themselves, to be confident and independent, to discover and manifest their abilities, to live without fear and injustice, to be able to meet responsibilities and, 'since liberty should not be austere, have their fling when they feel like it'.

It was that kind of socialism that won me when I was very

young. And then, without much delay, it also became clear to me that the generosity of spirit and spending that gives life to such views required something more than kind thoughts and decent intentions. Those motives of compassion were – and are – irreplaceable. But unless they could be translated into tangibles like jobs and homes and care and security and opportunity they would be nice and nothing else. If the necessary provision was to be made it obviously had to be paid for. The means of doing that therefore had to be found. For some time it seemed to me that those resources already existed and were simply being kept by those who had more than enough of the good things. Like many others before and since I thought that spreading those good things around was mainly a matter of performing a gigantic Robin Hood act. Then, just as I settled down to certainty in that view – I must have been about 16 – some old socialists in my home town of Tredegar who had always been kind enough to answer my questions told me it wasn't quite like that. Taking from those that had more than enough in order to give to those in need was right, they said. But by itself it wasn't anything like sufficient to make even the basic provision that was needed, as long as it was needed, for all of the people who needed it. That was the reason, they explained (with some help from the Institute library that they used like a bookshelf) that socialism wasn't just about giving and taking, it was also about making. It was not just about distributing with justice; it was also about producing with efficiency. That imperative of meeting human need was also the reason for trying to get socialism into democratic power. Production, and the investment of money and effort in production, could then be planned and increased, and more of the wealth generated could serve the people.

I suppose that is where this book really came from. It was certainly the foundation of my view that democratic socialism is the politics of production, and the basis for a great deal of what I've thought and said and done in the years since those long conversations.

During that time the need for consistent policies to promote production has increased. The need for the modernization of machines and methods has grown greater. The need for government to be involved in leading expansion, backing industrial development and sponsoring research and training has been made more clear by the successful example of rival nations. Those needs are now more intense and more obvious than ever; but there is no constructive response from Mrs Thatcher's government. Its fiscal and monetary policies have continually combined to crush manufacturing. The absence of policies for industry and trade have simply helped our competitors to gain markets here in Britain and in the world economy. And when the case is put for the government initiatives that are essential to any modern economy, it raises the cry of 'Statism' and refuses to address the practical requirements of survival. Much of the economy and millions of the people of Britain have suffered terribly because of that attitude and the wilful acts of omission and commission that come from it. They can only ensure that matters get worse. Neglect has no way of making anything better.

That is why the alternatives that I put in this book are essential. All of the themes and many of the words that you will find here are those that I've used over several years in speeches and statements before audiences as varied as the Engineering Employers Federation, the Association of Liberal Education, the Manchester Business School, the National Federation of Self Employed and Small Businesses, the Institute of Careers Officers, the Science Policy Foundation, the American and Canadian Chambers of Commerce, the Industrial Society, the Trades Union Congress and many other conferences and seminars inside and outside the Labour Movement. Not surprisingly, the proposals and arguments which I put in this book and elsewhere are consistent with the policies of my Party. Heresy hunters will therefore search in vain.

Over the years that I have been making the case for the policies of production I have been helped and advised by many friends and, though they won't be pleased, some foes too. Among the friends have been managers and shop stewards, members of workers' co-ops, teachers, technicians, scientists, economists in universities and in business, councillors trying to bring jobs to their area, company directors working for expansion. I give them my thanks and I offer gratitude, too, to the people of the Labour Movement for their support and determination to win, to my staff for their untiring work and great loyalty and to my family for their understanding and their love.

Neil Kinnock
London, September 1986

1
Rebuilding Britain

The Conservative government's first job will be to rebuild our economy and unite a divided and disillusioned people.
Conservative Party Manifesto, 1979

In Britain, the five years after the Second World War brought remobilization for peace, a great impetus towards repair and recovery from the conflict, and major institutional and owner-ship changes. In the following decade the buoyancy of demand, the residual strengths of production and the slow growth of competition gave a sense of security which obscured the need – or at least impeded the will – to make fundamental changes. By the late fifties and early sixties, however, the warnings of the penalties for failing to change were beginning to be heeded. A planning consensus developed around the recognition that new investment in labour and capital productivity was required. Regional development, technological promotion and educa-tional reform policies were started. In crisis and without calcula-tion, devaluation came to give stimulus, stayed to give a little respite, and then was lost in a lack of response.

In the early seventies, the Heath government went through a sort of Thatcherite adolescence before recanting on the policies which had taken unemployment to a million and going on a re-flationary spending spree.

Membership of the EEC was, throughout this period,

1

advertised as offering a sort of contagious success. Tariff-free access to the Common Market countries, it was argued, would offer Britain one-way trade advantages, or a 'cold shower' of competition, or communicable Germanic virtues, or even all three, depending on which speaker was addressing which audience.

By the mid-seventies alarm bells were really ringing as oil shocks and continuing poor performance dragged the economy towards stagnation. A minority government tried to respond with policies for investment, training, employment, relocation and reorientation of capital and labour, cost reduction, trade promotion and advocacy of international commercial reform and economic expansion. It was forced instead to operate policies of contraction. For its pains it was dumped – either because it was too mean towards the workers or because it was too soft towards the workers, or because it was too conciliatory or because it was provoking conflict – or for all these conflicting reasons and a few others besides. Anyway, it was said to be 'not working'. And the party which said that came into power and promptly set about breaking all 'not working' records.

The arctic blast of Thatcherite clumsiness and callousness in the early eighties made Heath's 'cold shower' of the early seventies seem in retrospect to have been a Turkish bath. Business and employment crashed. Those years of stupidity and malice, unemployment, waste and decline should and could have brought merciless punishment from the electorate. They didn't. The public's reaction to two wars – a real one in the Falklands and an apparent one in the Labour Party – saved the Government from political defeat while another factor, a more important factor, blunted the effects of their economic policies and consequently muted the wrath of the electorate.

They had the oil. Mrs Thatcher's government survived on oil. It provided revenues that sustained solvency when other sources of production, sale and income were being wiped out. It provided funds without which unemployment would have been

2

even greater, poverty even deeper, taxes even higher, cuts even bigger. The oil enabled the fiction of economic 'recovery' to be backed by the odd shadow of statistical fact as private household borrowing shot to record levels and credit relaxation gave a short spurt to the economy. Most of all, the oil bonus put off the day of economic reckoning which has been brought closer and made bleaker by the scrapyard economic policies of the Thatcher years.

But the reckoning has come nonetheless. Now there is no post-war impetus, no soft market, no shortage of foreign competition. Devaluation can be an instrument to assist a range of other recovery policies, but it cannot provide a haven against the realities of our investment, production and trade position. The markets of the EEC are manifestly not open doors to a life-giving sales boom, and our accumulated weaknesses deriving from underinvestment mean that the pressures coming from producers in partner countries are more likely to squeeze than to stimulate.

The oil is going. There is no more breathing space, no time to be bought; gentle decline has turned into a ruinous dive. Now there is no option other than investment and training for our future; no course other than producing and selling. Now we must be making our way.

ESTABLISHING PRIORITIES

The government's current view of our economic condition is a curious blend of complacency and pessimism. Obeisance to the power of 'market forces' dictates the simultaneous claims that everything is fine, and that if it's not fine, nothing can be done anyway.

I don't think everything is fine. Neither do I accept that nothing can be done. On the contrary, I believe that our situation is very bad and getting worse, that much must be done, and that it must be done now. I further believe that the action must be guided by four propositions:

3

- First, there is no prospect of a sustainable reduction in unemployment in this country unless we can attain stable long-term economic growth.
- Secondly, there is no possibility of long-term growth and resilient prosperity for the British economy without a major development of British manufacturing industry.
- Thirdly, the length of our relative economic decline, and the way in which it has been accelerated and intensified in the past seven years presents our country with a new set of strategic problems to which we must find new strategic answers.
- Fourthly, none of the major social, commercial, industrial or employment problems that we face is self-correcting. If they are to be overcome, systematic, planned action must be taken by the government in concert with all participants in the economy to construct that framework of economic, educational, technical and social conditions within which we can secure the necessary change, and within which the economy can thrive.

The central theme of all that follows is that we must build our economic policy around the recovery of manufacturing industry. Industrial policy will not be just one of the parts of Labour's economic strategy. It will be at the very core. That course will be obviously and radically different from the one taken by the present government which, insofar as it has any industrial strategy at all, seems to base it on the premise that Britain can somehow be shrivelled into solvency.

The new approach requires a change from the policy convention that lasted from the forties to the seventies, by which, under governments of both parties, policy was generally and chiefly formulated in overall, aggregated terms. Governments sought to determine the overall level of economic activity – the overall level of employment, the overall balance of payments position – while the *composition* of output as between manufactures and services, the *composition* of our trade, the *composition* of employment, were matters of lesser concern. At times it looked as if the attitude was: 'We'll look after the aggregates and the working parts will look after themselves'.

That is not to say, of course, that important industrial policies were not implemented, and it does not imply that governments should be careless of those overall considerations. Nor am I suggesting that the new economic policy requires a government finger in every pie – far from it. But since we now face the loss of oil production and revenues and since manufacturing industry has been subject to such contraction as a source of output, trade, income and employment, it is essential to consider the question of composition in order to focus stimulation and support for investment, research and design, training, marketing, and much else. A strategy that depended simply on a generalized stimulation of demand coupled with a hope that such a boost would launch and sustain both recovery and reform would be aimless and wasteful.

Prudence and practicality therefore require that we establish priorities for the use of resources, and that we make those priorities dependable for public and private industries and services and those who manage and work in them, by planning their use. And since we face the dual challenge of simultaneously combatting slump now and fostering the structural changes necessary to stop and reverse long-term deficiencies and decline, planning must have a dual perspective too. The policies that we implement immediately must be consistent with the objective of promoting the structural change. The policies that fight unemployment and underinvestment and trade loss in the late eighties must be part of a sustained strategy to make us fit for the future.

This approach must apply to decisions relating to the medium- and long-term planning needs of industries and the conflicting short-term pressures that conventionally come from the Treasury. It must apply to our education and training systems, to support for research and development, to communications, housing and construction. It must apply, indeed, in all considerations of consumption and investment.

5

The insistence on priorities must not become an excuse for postponement; if it did the strategy would lose respect and credibility. What is necessary, therefore, is an understanding that the need for action is immediate, that the need for provision is immense, that the means available are limited, that the priorities chosen will consequently have to be particular and that the pursuit of those priorities will have to be persistent. There can be changes of pace, but the direction must consistently and unerringly be towards economic recovery and structural reform. In that way there will be gradual but perceptible proof that the programme of priorities is a strategy for continual and coherent action and not an alibi for inaction.

The approach is restrained. It has to be. It is not so by preference, but because of the imperatives of reality. Chief among those are the immensity of demands and the comparative paucity of resources, and the fact that in the Thatcher years the *needs* of our society have been hugely increased whilst, as a result of the self-same policies, the *means* of producing wealth to meet those needs have ruinously decreased. It was clear after the first six months of the Thatcher government that its legacy would be multiplied misery, subtracted strength, a divided society and added difficulty. It was clear, too, that such an inheritance would have major implications for what the Labour Party could promise and what an incoming Labour government could do. I did not make myself popular in some quarters by pointing out the obvious at the time. Now, after some seven years of continued crumble, there can be few who do not recognize the scale of the devastation and realize its significance for the next Labour government. To make that recognition is not to be intimidated, it is to be challenged.

The question is, how do we rise to that challenge? Is it enough to rage against the injustice and waste in our country which should infuriate any conscious citizen, let alone a socialist? Or is it not obvious that the challenge is not to our emotions, but to our ability to understand the size of the task and the shortage of the tools, and still get on with the job of building and bettering our country? That certainly is the toughest course, requiring responsiveness to conditions as well as fidelity to convictions. But it is the only course for anyone who is serious about securing advances in employment, freedom and equality for and with the British people.

It is certainly the course that I shall take, and it is obvious that throughout the Labour Movement the great majority is set upon that approach too. The purpose of our ends and our means is not to gain the commendation of conservatives by being cautious, it is to earn the trust and sustained support of our fellow citizens by the realism of our approach and the reality of our achievements. That is the way to help our country to work its way out of decline, insecurity and injustice. And it is the only feasible means of making a secure foundation for socialism in Britain. 'At the moment,' wrote Aneurin Bevan in *In Place of Fear* (1952),

> we are between two worlds. We have lost the propulsions of one and we have not yet gained the forward thrust of the other. This is no place in which to halt. That is not to say a halting place cannot be reached. I think it can. It is clear to the serious student of modern politics that a mixed economy is what most people of the West would prefer. The victory of socialism need not be universal to be decisive. I have no patience with those Socialists, so-called, who in practice would socialise nothing while in theory they threaten the whole of private property. They are purists and therefore barren.

In the 35 years since, the 'propulsions' have still failed to generate the growth or guarantee the justice necessary for a satisfactory, let alone a socialist, society. We are plainly not at a place to halt, either in Thatcherism or in barren purity. The former is destroying our country, the latter would destroy our cause. Our duty to both is to get on with achieving that 'forward thrust', attaining the decisive victories of socialism. And the precondition of that is that we once again prove in practice, by our use of democratic power in government, the humanity and efficiency of our values, our policies and our priorities.

7

2
Mrs Thatcher's Legacy: No Foundations

There has been the odd report recently that Thatcherism has run its course, and is on its way out. As an informed source close to Downing Street, I have to report that those reports are eyewash. We're only just beginning. We've barely got past the stage of excavation. . . .

Margaret Thatcher, 15 March 1986

Britain's oil boom got under way in earnest in 1979. It ended seven years later, in 1986, when the price of oil fell by half, production reached its peak and the long, inevitable decline in oil output began.

That unrepeatable flood of riches, that unique opportunity, coincided almost exactly with Margaret Thatcher's tenure of the office of Prime Minister.

LUCKY BRITAIN

In 1979, after years of intensive exploration and development, the hazardous task of raising oil in the hostile waters of the North Sea began to pay off. Production was now on stream. From only 12 million tonnes produced in 1976, output had leapt

8

to 78 million tonnes in 1979. Five years later, annual production had risen to 121 million tonnes, and Britain was second only to Saudi Arabia as an exporter of oil to the markets of the world. Our luck was extraordinary. Not only did we have the obvious boon of the black gold itself, but our oil arrived at just the time when the price of oil hit a peak. It was like winning the pools just when the first dividend was doubled.

In 1973, at the time of the first oil price rise, Britain – along with all the other non-oil-producing countries – had suffered a severe drop in income both because we now had to buy expensive oil from OPEC and because of the disruption that the oil price rise caused to trade and production throughout the industrialized world. In 1979, too, there was disruption, and the industrialized world slipped into a major depression in 1981. But this time we were on the other side of the fence. The rise in the oil price meant a transfer of income *from* the rest of the world *to* us. The French, the Germans, the Italians and the Japanese have virtually no domestically produced oil, and the United States does not produce enough to cover its own needs. So while all our major industrial competitors suffered cuts in real income as they were forced to pay higher prices for their oil imports, we in Britain could enjoy the bumper revenues from oil exports.

The oil boom went from strength to strength. From 1979 to 1983 growth in the output of oil was virtually the only contributor to the growth of our national economy. By 1985 oil was contributing £18,000 million a year to our balance of payments and £12,000 million a year to the Treasury in taxes.

The government had always known that it would all come to an end one day. But it was totally unprepared for what happened. In January 1986 the oil price was halved. Instead of income being distributed *towards* oil producers, as in the past, it was distributed *away* from them. A feeling grew in some quarters in Europe and America that perhaps the decade of instability and recession, of inflation and rising unemployment, was over at last, and a new era of industrial expansion was about to begin. Even in Britain, one of the countries that was losing out

9

from the fall in the oil price, the more short-sighted commentators clutched desperately at this new optimism. After all, wasn't Britain still, in spite of everything, a major industrial country? Surely Britain would benefit from the industrial upswing too?

Facts, sadly, were too strong for this rather shallowly rooted hopefulness. Britain began to lose revenues as a result of the fall in oil prices, and – far more damaging – output of oil ceased to grow. A cut in the *price* may encourage expansion elsewhere and so make market conditions generally more buoyant. A fall in *output* benefits no-one and costs Britain dear. From this point on, be it ever so slowly, it was going to be downhill all the way.

Of course, there is still a lot of oil in the North Sea. Britain will not be self-sufficient much beyond 1990. There may be new discoveries to boost revenues above what is currently expected. And the great boom, the boom that brought £55,000 million in revenue to the Treasury in those seven years, is over.

Where did all the money go?

WASTE

For many it's difficult to remember what the British economy was like before Margaret Thatcher became Prime Minister. In May 1979 there were 1,250,000 unemployed. That was far too many, but the numbers were *falling* and had been falling for nearly a year. In May 1986 unemployment, as now measured, reached 3,400,000. Moreover, in the meantime, the way in which unemployment is measured has been changed no fewer than 16 times. Some of the changes were genuine statistical tidying. But most were made with the purpose and the consequence of bringing down the jobless figures without touching unemployment. By these devices the government has successfully 'reduced' the number of unemployed by about 500,000.

Not only has the number of unemployed increased, so has the average length of time spent on the dole. In May 1979, there were 340,000 long-term unemployed, that is, people un-employed for more than a year; 25 per cent of total unemployment. Now, even on the government's 'revised' method of counting, there are 1,400,000 long-term unemployed – 40 per cent of the total. Today, more people are forced to spend a year or more on the dole than were unemployed in total when Margaret Thatcher took office.

The reason for this terrible waste of lives is, of course, that the economy has performed very badly indeed under the Thatcher government. If the economy grows slowly it fails to create jobs, and the British economy has grown more slowly over the past seven years than in any period since the war. The average annual growth rate, *including the contribution of oil*, from 1979 to 1985 was a miserable 0.9 per cent. And if we dig beneath the surface of overall statistics to look at what has happened to one sector of our economy, our manufacturing industry, we uncover a yet more dismal scene.

Seven years after Margaret Thatcher took office, the level of output in British manufacturing industry is still 6 per cent *below* the level it was on the day she became Prime Minister. Investment in manufacturing industry is 18 per cent *below* the level of seven years ago. And 1,800,000 jobs have been lost in manufacturing industry – two-thirds of the total increase in unemployment.

The idle workers and the idle machinery, productive resources that could be turning out goods which would raise the standard of living of us all, are simply wasted. And the waste accumulates. Idle workers lose the skills they acquired when in work; idle machines are scrapped and not replaced. In 1981, 1982 and 1983 the Central Statistical Office reported that net investment in British manufacturing industry was *negative*. In other words, in those years, the scrapping was greater than the building. The skills and the machines which make up Britain's capacity to produce are shrinking.

Investing in the future involves investing in people and in ideas as well as machines. Here too, the story of recent years is one of cutback, closure and waste. Companies, desperate to cut costs, cut back on training and research. In 1983, the most recent year for which we have figures, only 40,000 apprentices started in British industry – down from 120,000 in 1979. In that same year, 1983, 620,000 apprentices were started in West Germany. British research budgets were cut too. Expenditure on research and development in Britain as a whole stagnated between 1979 and 1986; in manufacturing industry, R & D spending actually fell.

And the education system itself has been severely damaged. From underfunded primary schools, through equipment-starved secondary schools staffed by demoralized teachers, to universities and polytechnics struggling with reduced teaching budgets and seeing their best staff leave to seek better research facilities abroad, the education system is being starved, neglected, thrown away.

Apparently, we can't afford education, or training, or research, or investment. Despite all that oil money, we can't afford a future for our children.

WHAT WENT WRONG?

This tale of economic decay demands an explanation. How could a country which has suddenly enjoyed the most remarkable windfall suffer, virtually simultaneously, such a rapid economic decline?

A number of explanations suggest themselves:

- That this decline is merely the culmination of years of steady relative decline, dating back at least to the end of the Second World War, and perhaps even as far back as to the 1870s when Britain started to lose world economic supremacy to the United States and to Germany.
- That Britain's experience is no different from that of other

Western industrial countries. In the seventies all Western countries suffered a marked slowdown in economic growth compared with the fifties and sixties. All underwent a sharp recession in 1981 from which the European economies have made but a slow, tortuous recovery. (The Americans and the Japanese have done rather better, at least as far as cutting unemployment is concerned.)

- That the oil itself was the problem, a curse in disguise which so distorted the operation of our economy that all the advantages which it might have brought were lost in the costs of 'adjustment' to the new circumstances.
- That the government pursued foolish and inefficient policies, policies which not only failed to identify correctly the economic needs of the country but also were downright damaging. Policies, in other words, which wasted our oil, which threw away our chance for a better future.

Of course, all of these factors may have contributed something to the final outcome, and each must be examined in turn. But it is the last one, government policy, which must be examined in the greatest detail. For if errors were made, be they errors of omission or commission, then we must expose them and learn from them. Nothing in economic affairs is inevitable. Economic phenomena are not pre-ordained. They are not physically given characteristics of the universe. Economic organization is the product of social and political choices. If things are going wrong, then it is because wrong choices have been made.

Long-run decline

The proposition that Britain's current plight is simply a further stage in a long-run decline is distinctly unconstructive. Certainly, any serious policymaker must have historical perspective; but blaming 'history' merely shifts the problem back a stage. How then is that history to be explained – by the penalties of being the first industrial nation? By the focus on

Empire? By stupid policies? By the British character, which having shown a remarkable propensity for flexibility, innovation and social mobility in the first half of the nineteenth century suddenly underwent a 180-degree turn?

It's not difficult to see that Britain's spectacular economic success in the industrial revolution has played a part in our subsequent decline relative to later arrivals on the industrial scene. In the first hundred years or so of industrialization, the institutional structure of much of our modern economy was born. The peculiar position of the financial sector in the British economy; the structure of the relationship between finance and industry; the structure of industrial relations; the structure and content of education and training – all these institutional elements are products of our successful past and are contributing to our unsuccessful present. This is why it is important that in our current desperate position we should try to think about our economic future with an understanding of the past but without being encumbered by it. The simple fact that things have always been done in a particular way is no reason why they should be the same in the future. In practice the past will always lean heavily upon us; all the more reason, then, why it should not cramp our minds.

The more recent history of our decline since the end of the Second World War deserves far more detailed consideration than I can give it here. Suffice it to say that at the end of the war Britain had the opportunity to recover her economic vitality, to become an economic leader once again. Of course there had been enormous destruction, there were still huge bills to pay, and we had to learn to live in a world in which we would play second fiddle, politically and economically, to the Americans. But our other main competitors were prostrate.

The years of reconstruction under the Labour government of Clem Attlee are generally regarded as having been a qualified success. Mistakes were made, of which the premature return to a convertible pound in 1947 was the most important. It might be argued, too, that the devaluation of 1949 was inappropriate.

But the positive achievements, particularly in industrial policy, laid the foundations for enduring prosperity. Most important of all, in six years, by means of public spending, Clem Attlee's government created three-and-a-half million civilian jobs.

The Attlee government is usually remembered today for its great contributions to social reform – the creation of the welfare state and of the National Health Service – and for the nationalization and reconstruction of declining, decrepit and under-capitalized industries – coal, the railways, steel and so on. But more general industrial reorganization was made possible under the 1947 Industrial Organization and Development Act, the powers of which proved to be of particular importance in the rationalization of the textile industry.

In his book *Years of Recovery: British Economic Policy, 1945–51*, the distinguished economic historian, Sir Alec Cairncross, summed up the Labour government's performance:

> All in all, the early post-war years presented the government with a much more difficult task of economic management than the two decades that followed; and its mastery of that task entitled the government to all the more credit. It pointed the economy in the right direction, rode out the various crises that the years of transition almost inevitably gave rise to, and by 1951 had brought the economy near to eventual balance. No doubt there were false starts, concentration on secondary issues, a slowness to react, an unwillingness to act with sufficient firmness, and at the end a serious error over the scale of rearmament that was feasible. There was, too, little success in changing long-standing attitudes in industry that slowed down innovation and expansion. But whether one tries to look forward from 1945 or backwards from forty years later, those years appear in retrospect, and rightly so, as years when the government knew where it wanted to go and led the country with an understanding of what was at stake.[1]

The Tory governments elected from 1951 introduced a marked change of direction. They did not choose to understand what was at stake. Industrial structure was no longer to be a predominant concern of government. That could be left to the market. The task of government was merely to maintain a full-employment level of overall demand in the economy by manipulating taxes and government expenditure, and keeping interest rates at a suitable level.

This was the era of stop–go. The economy seemed to lurch between periods of growing optimism and balance-of-payments crises. When Tories claim that 'you've never had it so good', economic disaster cannot be far behind; and by the early sixties even the Tories realized that something was going badly wrong. Despite the undoubted rise in living standards it was clear that Britain was doing significantly worse than her main competitors. France, West Germany and Japan were all growing more rapidly, and were capturing markets which traditionally had been British. The Tory response was to attempt to import pale, powerless imitations of the French planning system. This belated recognition of the importance of industrial planning was a move in the right direction – but it was totally lacking in conviction.

In 1964 Labour, after 13 years of Toryism, inherited an economy once again afflicted with severe balance-of-payments problems, and with the signs of industrial backwardness becoming ever more evident. In the manifesto produced for the general election of that year it was argued that the main economic objectives of the Party – full employment and a faster rate of industrial expansion – could not be achieved 'by leaving the economy to look after itself'. For the first time in more than a decade there was a government in office committed to the modernization of British industry. And despite what we now know to have been an over-reaction to the financial crisis of 1966, the Labour government kept to that commitment. The new system of investment grants, together with the provisions of the Science and Technology Act of 1965 and the Industrial Expansion Act of 1968 did begin, at last, to raise the rate of investment in British industry.

16

The most effective economic institution in this period was the Industrial Reorganization Corporation (the IRC) set up in 1966. The IRC was given two tasks: the reorganization and development of existing industries, and the establishment and development of new industrial enterprises. The IRC soon assembled a highly competent and effective management team, and began to display the characteristics of the successful investment banks found in European countries and in Japan.

The Tory government elected in 1970 took office committed to the pursuit of the policies of 'Selsdon Man', an early version of Thatcherism. The Heath government promptly dismantled the most effective institutions of Labour's industrial policy, in particular abolishing the IRC. But the folly of Tory economic policy was soon exposed by a sharp increase in the rate of unemployment. Selsdon Man died a quick death and was replaced by Anthony Barber's 'dash for growth' – a wild spending spree that sucked in imports at a prodigious rate. Then there was the second miners' strike and the three-day week.

Labour returned to power to receive yet another 'poisoned chalice'; not only had the industrial base of the country been weakened by Tory incompetence, but the oil price rise of 1973 had thrown the industrial world into confusion. The United States, Germany and France deflated their economies hard, willing to see unemployment increase if only their balance-of-payments positions were secure. The Labour government attempted to protect jobs and paid the price of swimming against the deflationary tide. Yet despite the ramifications of the financial crisis of 1976 – which, now that all the figures are available, we know was nothing like as severe as was believed at the time – Labour did manage to protect jobs. The average increase in the rate of unemployment in Britain in the period 1974–9 was *less* in Britain than in France and Germany. And in 1979, when Labour left office, unemployment had been falling for more than a year.

But in retrospect, some of the most important economic achievements of that Labour administration were in industrial policy. Operating in the most difficult circumstances the Labour government, acting mainly through the National Enterprise Board, ensured the survival of the motor-car, machine-tool and computer industries in this country, and laid the foundations of our information technology and biotechnology industries. However, most important of all and for the first time since 1950, the fall in Britain's share of the world market in manufactured goods was at last halted. Our share of the world market was 5 per cent higher when Labour left office than when we were elected – the only government since Attlee's that could boast such an achievement.

Nonetheless, despite the achievements of the Labour governments, the overall picture of the post-war economy is one of steady decline. The constructive industrial policies introduced by successive Labour governments have been frustrated repeatedly by short-term financial problems, particularly problems associated with the balance of payments. As a backbencher I attacked the Labour government's acceptance of expenditure cuts dictated by the IMF in 1976 and also the restrictions placed on the National Enterprise Board. I was acting then on instinctive commitment to production, not with the knowledge we now have that the true economic and financial situation was far better than the figures then suggested.

Of course, the economic performance of the fifties, sixties, and seventies looks distinctly rosy when compared with the disasters of the past seven years. Even in the difficult years from 1974 to 1979, the Labour government achieved an average annual growth rate of 1.4 per cent, half as much again as that achieved in the oil-rich first six years of the Thatcher government. But in the long-term perspective of post-war development it can be seen that our performance was persistently worse than that of our major competitors. And it was this deficiency which steadily eroded the ability of the British economy to maintain full employment.

The complaint is frequently heard from industrialists and managers not making a partisan point that economic policy since the war has been like a pendulum swinging from side to side as one party or the other is in office – investment schemes introduced and then scrapped, industrial policy to the fore, then neglected, industries nationalized and then denationalized. The lack of consistency of objective and of policy has created instability and uncertainty, and has militated against the long-term planning which is the key to successful and sustained industrial expansion. I have considerable sympathy with this complaint. But I think that any objective examination of the record will show that the Labour Party has repeatedly found itself in the position of picking up the pieces after Tory mis-management has once again eroded the strength of our industry. In these circumstances there had to be a change of direction. I believe that I am not making a partisan point when I say that what we must learn from the experience of economic policy from 1945 to 1979 is the necessity for all governments of putting industrial policy *first*. I also believe that the Thatcher years have not been a mere continuation of the same sad tale. They have been something far worse.

A common fate?

The 1979 oil price rise, and the dollar crisis that accompanied it, triggered off a recession in all the major industrial countries. If Britain's performance had then simply paralleled that of its major competitors, that alone would have been a cause for con-siderable criticism of the government. After all, they are all oil importers while we are an oil exporter. But the remarkable fact is that on every measure of economic performance Britain has done *worse* in this period than the United States, France, Germany, Japan and Italy.

The average rate of growth from 1979 to 1985 was but 0.9 per cent in Britain; in France it was 1.1 per cent, in Italy 1.3 per cent, in West Germany 1.1 per cent, in the United States 2.1 per cent, and in Japan 4.3 per cent. The government is fond of point-ing out that Britain's growth rate since 1981 has been higher than that of other European countries. The choice of 1981 and not 1979 is, of course, quite deliberate, since it allows them to measure growth from the depths of a recession far worse than that experienced by other European countries.

Our poor growth performance is, as might be expected, reflected in poor unemployment figures. Britain has the highest unemployment rate of the six major industrial countries. Moreover, in Britain unemployment has increased 2.4 times over since 1979, as against 2.25 times in West Germany, 1.6 times in France, 1.5 times in Italy, and 1.3 times in Japan and the United States. And whereas unemployment in all the other five countries is now falling, in Britain it is *still rising*.

Finally, while all our competitors have, broadly speaking, managed to hold on to their shares of world trade in manufactures (with France, Italy and Germany suffering falls of the order of 10 per cent apiece, at the expense of gains by Japan and the United States), Britain has seen her share in world trade in manufactures fall every year since 1980, registering a cumulative fall of 22 per cent. The familiar slide which Labour had managed to halt in the seventies has resumed with a vengeance.

So, while it is obvious that Britain's economic performance over the past seven years has been worse than it would have been if the rest of the world had been enjoying a boom, we cannot blame those dreadful years on the rest of the world. Nor can we claim that we have simply shared in a global downturn. Britain's performance has been significantly worse than the rest – just at the time when North Sea oil should have enabled us to do far better.

A 'curse in disguise'?

A significant factor in economic debate over the past seven years has been the manner in which the ostensibly non-aligned Treasury has spent a good deal of time and energy in partisan support of the Thatcher government's cause. One of its more ingenious concoctions has been the idea that our problems are actually *due to* the oil boom; that the evident decline in manufacturing industry is the 'automatic result' of the growth of oil exports, and that the increase in unemployment with which the decline has been accompanied has been caused by a lack of 'flexibility' on the part of the labour force (for some reason employers are deemed to be sufficiently 'flexible') in adjusting to the changes that the oil boom has required.

The argument goes like this. In the long run the value of a country's exports must be roughly the same as the value of its imports. If exports were greater than imports for years and years, this would mean that the country was voluntarily enduring a lower standard of living than would be the case if it were willing to spend its high export earnings on imports. But if imports were for many years higher than exports, then a country would not be paying its way in the world. Eventually its credit would run out and it would have to cut its standard of living.

These commonplace relationships have, however, been stretched by the Tory government to account for the destruction of manufacturing industry and the deficit in manufactured trade over the years of their oil-rich rule. If exports and imports must, overall, be roughly equal (they say), then increased exports of one commodity must be balanced by increased imports of other commodities. So, if the discovery and exploitation of oil reserves in the North Sea results in a surplus on our trade in oil, then a deficit must emerge in the trade of other sectors of the economy. The appearance of Britain's first ever deficit on manufactured trade, and the huge loss of jobs and companies in manufacturing, is then the 'natural' concomitant of the new surplus in the oil trade.

The 'natural' mechanism which directs this outcome is the movement of the exchange rate. The surplus on trade in oil puts upward pressure on the pound. The pound rises against the dollar, and against the currencies of our European competitors and of Japan. The high exchange rate makes manufactures uncompetitive. A deficit appears in trade in manufactures, and this deficit grows and grows until the impact of the oil surplus on the overall account is balanced by an equal and opposite deficit in manufactured goods.

This tale had a hideous credibility in 1981, when it was evident that the competitive position of British manufacturing industry was being hopelessly undermined by the high value of the pound. But, apart from that trauma, the Treasury's tale does not stand up to careful examination.

First, the balance-of-payments account is made up of items other than trade in oil and trade in manufactures. In particular, there is trade in services. The goverment has often claimed that Britain's future lies in the export of services, and has built reassurance out of the surplus which the service sector earns in international trade. What it has failed to explain is why it should have been manufacturing which fell to their inexorable laws of trading arithmetic, and not services. Why was the surplus on oil account not matched in part or in whole by a deficit on trade in services?

Once the question is asked, it is evident that the answer must be found in the characteristics of many of the service industries, their competitiveness in the markets in which they trade, their record for innovation, their marketing skills, and the investment made in maintaining those strengths. With some notable exceptions, British manufacturing industries did not have those attributes; and they were hammered. Their problems, in short, are problems inherent in the manufacturing industries themselves. They cannot be explained away as a regrettable but inevitable 'automatic' process.

Secondly, even though it is true that in the long run the balance of payments must balance, it can balance equally well in a boom as in a slump. It is virtually inevitable that higher levels of output and employment will be accompanied by higher levels of imports. Higher output requires more materials, many of which must be imported. And the higher incomes earned when more people are in work will be spent, in part, on imports. So if imports have to increase when a surplus appears on trade in oil, then why should not that increase in imports be the product of higher output and employment, rather than the cause of a shrinkage in both, as actually occurred?

The attempt to portray our oil fortune as a curse in disguise is either stupid, or wicked, or both. North Sea oil presented the British government with some golden opportunities. It didn't take them. It wasted them. Instead of rising to the challenge and taking the chances offered by the bonus, the government threw them away; and when the results of its fecklessness became obvious it turned to inventing alibis rather than taking remedial action.

Economic policy, Thatcher-style

Any government which, in the circumstances of the oil boom, failed to take steps to reverse Britain's long-term decline, failed to insulate Britain from some of the worst effects of the world recession, and failed to adapt its policies to take account of the impact of oil on the economy, would rightly be considered inefficient.

Any government which, in the most favourable economic circumstances faced by any government since the Second World War, presided over the worst slump that Britain has suffered since the thirties and allowed Britain's relative position in the world economy to deteriorate more rapidly than ever before must surely be judged unfit to rule.

Throughout the lifetime of that government the number of victims has increased. So has the number of critics. Some have said that the government didn't care; some have said that they didn't know. Neither view takes sufficient account of the fact that government policies have been deliberate to the point of didacticism. And the dogma which has guided those policies has been monetarism.

The theories of monetarism are founded on two basic propositions, both of which are wrong. The first proposition is that the rate of inflation in the economy is determined by the rate of growth of cash in circulation, of bank deposits, of credit, and so on; that is, of the money supply. Now, while it is sometimes true that prices and the amount of money move in the same direction, this doesn't help us much in deciding which is causing which. If you drive a car fast it uses more petrol. So fast driving and the supply of petrol go together. But you won't turn a Mini into a Jaguar by putting more petrol in the tank.

Despite such obvious problems of confusing connected events with cause and effect, some distinctly shabby statistical relationships between increases in the money supply and inflation were said to 'prove' the truth of the monetarist case. However, a pair of wise letter writers to *The Times* (4 April 1977) expressed some doubt about the usefulness of these statistical exercises. They pointed out that there was a closer relationship between variations in the rate of inflation and the fluctuating incidence of dysentery in Scotland, than there was between inflation and the growth of the money supply. Subsequent history has justified the letter writers' scepticism. The link between the growth of the money supply and the rate of inflation on which the monetarists based their case has been remarkably elusive. Try as they might – fiddle the statistics, redefine what the money supply is, change their monetary targets – nothing works; they can't find the relationship they seek.

The second proposition upon which monetarism is based is that the automatic working of a 'free' market will ensure an 'efficient' allocation of resources. By this is meant not merely that a competitive market will tend to reward the industrious and punish the lazy, but that the operations of the market will ensure that all resources are allocated 'efficiently' among alternative uses and that they are fully employed. So if only the market were given its head with the inhibitions and the inflexibilities removed there would be no unemployment problem, and no need to worry about the level of investment, or whether sufficient expenditure was going towards research and development, or whether sufficient skilled workers were being trained – the market would take care of our present and our future. And because the market will ensure that the economy is fully employed, variations in the money supply can only affect the price level; they can have no effect on output, for that is fixed already.

From here on the monetarists' economic policy takes on a manic logic. If the operations of the free market are so beneficial, then any problems in the economy must be due to inhibitions on its operation. Taxation is inhibiting the willingness of the rich to work and save, so their taxes must be cut to make them richer and provide them with greater incentives. Social security benefits, and the protection afforded the weakest members of the labour force by the Wages Councils and other 'safety-net' arrangements, depress the stimulus to work among the poor. So benefits must be removed to make them poorer and encourage them to stand on their own feet.

Unemployment, it is then argued, can only be due to workers 'pricing themselves out of work'. The Treasury is wheeled in once again to attempt to provide some statistical backing for this slogan, and once again only succeeds in bringing discredit upon itself. Cutting wages will not increase employment. Whether workers are employed or not depends on whether someone is willing and able to buy what they produce at a remunerative price. Who would buy the goods that the extra workers, employed at lower wages, produced? The only sense that might be made of this argument is that lower costs might encourage exports. But the better way to lower costs is to increase efficiency by technical innovation, not enter into a futile wage-cutting war with countries such as Korea and Taiwan.

Moreover, those who suggest that British workers should 'price themselves into jobs' had better tell the British people whether they are willing to arrange an American situation in which 60 per cent of the unemployed get no benefit whatsoever and where the remaining 40 per cent who do get benefit receive payments that are worth 40 per cent or less of their previous earnings. I have the feeling that when faced with that obligation even the most ferocious wage-cutting prophet would find another gospel. I believe that the answer to the relationship between labour costs and employment possibilities lies not in the social *insecurity* strategy of reducing costs by cutting wages, but in the social *solidarity* strategy, as operated by the Japanese, of reducing costs by improving productivity.

Next, the free market argument is turned against the trades unions. Since no institutions must be allowed to restrict the workings of the market, trade unions, which exist in part to inhibit the exploitative effects of the market, must be weakened in any way possible. The same argument is not, however, extended to the case of large companies and to their role in inhibiting the operations of the 'free' market, since the pressures of 'competition' are thought to be enough to insure against the growth of corporate restrictive practices.

The 'free' market argument also justifies the attack on government expenditure. Since, it is argued, the government's activity is not directed and disciplined by the free play of market forces, whereas (in spite of all evidence to the contrary) private activities are so disciplined, then all public expenditure is a Bad Thing, and all private expenditure a Good Thing.

This opposition to public expenditure links up nicely with the abhorrence of any increase in the money supply. There is believed to be a link between government expenditure and the growth of the money supply. In fact, any such link is very roundabout, and no clear statistical relationship to underpin it has been found. But no amount of evidence will deflect the evangelical monetarist or the Tory ideologue in full flood. And so the key indicator in determining economic policy in Britain today is not the level of unemployment, or the rate of economic growth, or our trade performance, or the future prospects of our industry, but the public sector borrowing requirement – the PSBR – the excess of government expenditure over revenue.

If the consequences were not so sickening, the whole crazy edifice of theoretical ravings would make an excellent black comedy, a bizarre practical joke played on the real world by cloistered ivory-tower economists. But the sombre consequences of using the principles of old-fashioned economics as a basis for constructing practical policies have been all too evident in Britain in the past seven years.

Immediately it took office, in the face of the mounting world recession, the Thatcher government took action which simultaneously accelerated the inflation rate and raised the exchange rate. The increase in VAT and the raising of interest rates to 17 per cent and more crushed British industry in a brutal vice. Costs rose at home as wages responded to higher prices in the shops and high interest payments cut into cash flow. At the same time these high interest rates boosted the exchange rate which made British exports 25 per cent more expensive – and foreign imports into Britain 25 per cent cheaper. The result was the most calamitous collapse of British industry ever. Manufactured output fell by 15 per cent between 1979 and 1982, a depth from which it is still trying to claw its way back. The share of the home market captured by imports rose, and exports declined, with equal rapidity.

A further priority of the Thatcher government, in line once again with its free-market mania, was to remove all restrictions on the export of capital from Britain. This, they claimed, would lead to 'more efficient allocation of investment funds'. The result has certainly been a different allocation of investment. About £25,000 million of it has gone away from Britain, the main beneficiary of this bold gesture being Ronald Reagan. The outflow of capital from Britain has helped to finance his public-borrowing-led boom in investment, production, sales and jobs in the USA.

The £25,000 million that flowed out of Britain between 1979 and 1986 is about half the value of Britain's foreign earnings from the export of North Sea oil. Most of the money was invested by insurance companies and pension funds, which tripled the part of their assets held in foreign securities from about 5 per cent to more than 15 per cent.

Some industrial and commercial companies got in on the act too. Their investment in overseas financial assets in the period

27

1979–84 was double that in the period 1973–8. It wasn't that they had the money to spare. At the same time that they were putting money into other developed economies, their net investment in new productive capacity in Britain was being cut by more than half. Indeed, under the Thatcher government British industrial and commercial companies have spent more on buying financial assets overseas than they have on increasing their productive capacity at home.

In short, the Thatcher government has been willing, even eager, to see the revenues from North Sea oil invested overseas, instead of using them to modernize Britain's own industrial capacity, ready for the day when oil earnings from abroad should start to decline. In 1979, not even the most hostile forecaster of the effect of Thatcherism would have anticipated such sabotage of basic British interests. But it happened. It is continuing. And it will continue for as long as Mrs Thatcher's Tories rule.

Whatever one might say about the policies of the early Thatcher years – and all that can really be said about them is that they were disastrous for Britain – they were coherent in their callous, monetarist way. But as the years have dragged on the pretensions to coherence have fallen away.

Monetary policy has fallen apart completely as one monetary target after another has been abandoned. The government clings to the symbol of the PSBR, a statistic which all serious observers declare to be totally irrelevant to the operation of the real economy, and even totally irrelevant to monetary policy too. In a desperate attempt to feed the PSBR monster that it has itself created, the government has raised taxes – the share of personal incomes paid in taxes is now 44 per cent, compared with 37 per cent under the last Labour government – and it has borrowed more – around £60,000 million so far compared with £40,000 million borrowed in the five years of the last Labour administration, to say nothing of the additional sum of over £15,000 million it has raised by selling off state assets, all on top of the £55,000 million in revenues from the North Sea.

The damage that these frantic measures might do to British industry is simply ignored, as is the impact of historically high real interest rates, which are the government's only means of staving off the sterling crisis that repeatedly threatens as Britain's international trading performance steadily deteriorates.

The only tattered remnant of what was once paraded as a new, exciting set of political ideas is the old right-wing dogma that everything should be left to the operation of the 'free' market, whether it be the planning of Britain's future energy policy, the cleaning of hospital wards, the funding of university research, the management of our water supplies, the provision of nursery facilities or the BBC. Every aspect of life is squeezed into the same mean, dogmatic mould.

The notion of an efficient 'free' market should, in the interests of public health, hygiene and safety, be confined to the text books. If it is applied to the real world it becomes dangerous. The 'free' market is not capable of determining the volume of investment which will ensure a full employment level of demand today and adequate growth in the future. The 'free' market does not manage natural monopolies, such as gas and water, any more efficiently than it manages private monopolies. Its magic mechanisms do not provide the right amount of collaborative research in industry or the universities, permit efficient large-scale child care or medical services or schooling. And anyone who thinks that the 'free' market is the best arbiter in the arts and media might do well to spend some time watching American television.

In fact, the ideology of the 'free' market belittles the influence and usefulness of market institutions. The pretence that market forces can and should determine everything devalues the market. In a properly managed framework, the market has enormous power to stimulate innovation, to provide variety, to foster and reward initiative. The stultifying conformity and drab incompetence of the Eastern European economies are clear testimony to the value of market forces and the price paid for their elimination; just as unemployment, underinvestment, urban decay and bitter social division are the clear consequence of handing the economy over to an unmanaged market. Dogma, whether of Eastern European bureaucracies or Mrs Thatcher's monetarism, should have no place in the formation of economic policy.

The full consequences of the Tory substitution of the dogma of the free market for serious thought will become evident as the constructive argument proceeds in the rest of this book. My case up to now is that it has been the massive incompetence of Tory economic policy which has inflicted so much economic damage on this country in the past seven years. The oil has been wasted. Assets have been stripped. Unique opportunities have gone forever. The blame cannot be laid at the door of history, or the world slump, or the oil boom itself. It is Margaret Thatcher and her minions who must bear the blame.

THE TORY SUCCESSES

It would seem to be rather unfair to concentrate solely on the massive mess the Tories have made of economic policy in general, and to say nothing of the successes which they claim to have achieved. I am somewhat reluctant to do so, not because I am not prepared to give credit where it is due, but because my comments may appear somewhat carping and mean-minded. However, it is crucial to clear away the rosy clouds of Tory self-delusion if we are to formulate an effective strategy for Britain's economic recovery.

The biggest Tory boast is, of course, that they have conquered inflation. Carefully omitting any mention of their first two years in office, when inflation almost doubled, they point to the 3 per cent inflation rate of 1986 as a triumphant vindication of all the pain and suffering.

Before examining this claim, it is worth pointing out that the Tories did not argue, at first, that a low rate of inflation is an end in itself. A low rate of inflation, they declared, is the foundation of growth and expanding employment. If only we get inflation down, then all will be well. Since inflation has fallen and all is very obviously not well this earlier argument has taken a back seat.

But can the Tories claim that the rate of inflation has fallen as a consequence of their policies? Some suspicion may be raised by the fact that all other industrial countries have enjoyed the same fall in the inflation rate as we have in Britain, even without the dubious pleasure of a Thatcher government. Indeed, inflation in the other major industrial countries has fallen *more rapidly* than inflation in Britain, so that our inflation rate, relative to that of our competitors, is now *higher* than it was in 1979. What all industrial countries have enjoyed in common is a sharp fall in the prices of raw materials, especially oil. That is where we should begin to look for an explanation of the fall in inflation.

The implications of this point are quite appalling. If the fall in inflation has not been 'bought' by all the pain and suffering of the Thatcher years, if the fall in inflation would have happened anyway, then the whole ghastly exercise has been for nothing.

But the fall in inflation is not the only Tory 'success'. It is also claimed that British industry is now more efficient, 'leaner and fitter'. Support for this claim, when support is offered, is usually found in the upsurge in productivity growth in British industry which occurred from 1981 to 1983, when output per worker employed in British manufacturing rose by 7 per cent per year, the highest rate of growth in Europe. These were the same years in which net investment in British industry was negative. A curious combination of events, until it is realized that the productivity growth of those years was derived not from producing more goods with the same workers, but by producing fewer goods with many fewer workers. From 1979 to 1983 manufactured output fell by 16 per cent. Over the same period, employment in manufacturing fell by 23 per cent. Productivity 'growth' was a statistical sleight of hand. Relatively inefficient plant was being closed down and more efficient plant kept open, so that the average level of efficiency went up, but no new plant was being built to replace that which was being closed.

This degenerate form of productivity growth created by closure could not go on for too many years. Eventually, the closures had to slow down. And then the rate of productivity growth slowed down too. Britain's rate of productivity growth is now the lowest of the major industrial countries.

Whatever anecdotal 'evidence' beleaguered Tory politicians may think up to justify their claims of greater efficiency, they have to face the facts. If Britain is really more efficient as a result of their economic policies, then surely we should be capturing markets at home and abroad, or at very least holding our own. The sour reality is that we are losing markets both at home and abroad. Our share of world export markets is down by 22 per cent, and import penetration of our home market is up by 25 per cent.

One of the Tories' more outrageous claims of success is that they have 'created more jobs since 1983' (note the careful choice of starting date once again) 'than any other European country'. How can this be when unemployment continues to rise? An explanation may be sought in the increased number of people who are looking for work. Population growth has played a part. In addition people who would not previously have looked for work are now doing so either through choice or because they have been forced into the labour market through family poverty.

Looking at the figures for 'new jobs' produces a quite different explanation. First, each 'job' is counted as a separate employee, even if the same person is doing two jobs. So if a hard-up schoolteacher takes an evening job at the pub, then he or she is counted as an 'extra' employee. Secondly, *two-thirds* of all the *increase* in jobs is attributable to the Department of Employment's *estimate* of the increase in the number of self-employed, even though only *one-tenth* of the labour force taken as a whole is self-employed. The last time an accurate measure of the self-employed was made was in the census of 1981. Another accurate figure will not be produced until 1991. Meanwhile the Department of Employment uprates the figure for self-employment by 125,000 every year for no reason that they will explain. The source of this estimate is shrouded in mystery. In fact, it's just a guess. So whatever happens elsewhere in the economy, there will be 125,000 new (self-employed) 'jobs' every year. Thirdly, the increase in employees is composed of a sharp fall in full-time jobs, and a large increase in part-time jobs. The Bank of England, after careful statistical study of the average hours worked in part-time employment, converted the part-time jobs into 'full-time equivalents', i.e. one part-time job is roughly equal, in hours worked, to half a full-time job. When this correction is made to the employment figures it uncovers a small *fall* in the number of full-time equivalent jobs since 1983 rather than a substantial increase.

Surveying the Department of Employment's calculations, my colleague Gordon Brown commented that Lord Young's construction of the jobs figures is 'a feat equivalent to taking an appalling balance sheet, inflating assets, minimizing the liabilities and producing an annual report that has taken optimism to the point of fraud. Presentation is one thing, creative accounting another. But Lord Young's treatment of the job statistics amounts to the invention of a new category of computer crime.'[2]

Margaret Thatcher has sought to shrug off these damning facts by arguing that part-time work is a great boon to women and should not be denigrated. Quite right. Adequately paid part-time employment would be a great boon to anyone, man or woman, who wished or needed to arrange his or her life around that sort of job. But it is ridiculous to suggest that that is what has happened over the past seven years. What has really happened is that one family member has lost a full-time, properly paid job, and another family member has been forced to take poorly paid part-time work to make ends meet. The social and personal consequences of this alteration in the pattern of family work, inside and outside the home, amount not to progressive change, but to egregious cruelty. The Tory claim to be the 'party of the family' rings rather hollow in the homes of the unemployed.

Last, but by no means least, the Tories claim to have induced 'a new spirit of realism in industrial relations', to have made trade unions 'more democratic' and to have created conditions in which 'managers can manage'. Nobody would claim that industrial relations in Britain were perfect in the seventies, or at any previous time. Nobody would suggest that there were not useful reforms that could be made. But the Tory approach has been to stimulate social conflict, not social co-operation; to brow-beat workers, to treat them as 'the enemy within', to dismiss contemptuously their struggles to preserve their jobs and their communities.

This strategy will work in a slump. As long as there is more interest in firing than in hiring workers; as long as there is more interest in cutting investment than introducing new technologies; as long as new skills are not required; then the co-operation of the workers is not required. Industrial regimentation can replace industrial relations. But, as a glance at the industrial relations practices of our competitors in Japan and Germany will readily show, social co-operation is the keystone of successful industrial relations in a progressive, innovative society. Technical change is fostered by co-operation; conflict slows down the pace of change. The bitterness created by the Tories will retard our industrial recovery.

So, when examined with care, the Tory 'successes' amount to a mixture of dubious statistical constructions and bully-boy boasting. Instead of contributing to industrial expansion, the conquest of markets and the creation of jobs, they have derived from contraction, loss of markets, and the destruction of jobs.

We must tackle inflation. We must make British industry more competitive. We must provide more full-time and part-time jobs, properly paid jobs. We must create a modern industrial relations system. We must be efficient. There is no socialist virtue in inefficiency. To achieve these ends we must build to replace the ruins the Tories leave behind. I will argue that the key to doing that is to be found in the recovery of Britain's manufacturing industry.

The Thatcher government's mismanagement of Britain's economic affairs over the past seven years cannot be dismissed as simple incompetence. The waste of the oil, the wasting of our industries, the misery heaped upon the unemployed, the poor and the defenceless, the courting of the rich and unproductive, the antipathy to production – all this was no mistake. It was a deliberate, concerted strategy to create a different sort of society in Britain, a society of self-serving meanness, a subservient society. That cannot be tolerated.

NOTES

1   Alec Cairncross, *Years of Recovery: British Economic Policy, 1945–51* (Methuen, London and New York, 1985), p. 509.
2   Gordon Brown, 'The Great Thatcher Jobs Fraud', *The Times*, 22 October 1985.

3

Creating Jobs:
Employment and Production

Unemployment is one of the greatest mysteries of our time.
Margaret Thatcher, 11 March 1982

Unemployment is economically inefficient.

It is indefensible that people should be unemployed in Britain when there are obviously so many things that need to be done. Houses need building. Sick people need nursing. Children need teaching. Steel, motor-cars, dishwashers, vacuum cleaners, central heating systems, need producing. Books need printing. Music needs playing. Everything that provides the material basis for a decent life.

The standard of living of the British people is only 80 per cent of that of the French, 70 per cent of that of the Germans and 60 per cent of that of the Americans. It will soon be lower than that of the Italians. To raise British living standards to the levels enjoyed by our fellow Western democracies requires a massive effort of production. Without that effort, levels of private consumption and the standard of provision of public services will not only remain below those of other countries, but will tend to fall relative to other countries. How stupid, then, that potential production is being wasted on the dole.

People who are unemployed are people who are being wasted.

Their own lives are cramped, constrained, unfree. The society in which they live is diminished materially and socially. The increase in unemployment under the Tories was the fundamental reason why the number of British people living in poverty increased from the dreadful figure of 6.1 million in 1979 to 8.9 million just four years later – more than one person in six. It is not in the least surprising to find that unemployment kills. Research in the United States has suggested that an increase of 1 million in the number of unemployed will lead to approximately 10,000 extra deaths every year. Studies by my colleagues Michael Meacher and John Prescott have produced similar results. An extra 1 million unemployed will result in more deaths every year than the annual toll due to road accidents.

A society in which a high level of unemployment is the normal state of affairs is a society without true freedom or fairness. Those who enjoy the prosperity and fulfilment of comfortable incomes and satisfying jobs when others are unemployed know that they are lucky. The inequality that is unemployment divides, vulgarizes and depresses the entire community.

The reduction of the level of unemployment is the predominant aim of the Labour Party and will be the over-riding objective of the next Labour government. Our ultimate goals must be an economy which provides a job for everyone who wants one, and a society in which people want to work, want to contribute, want to participate.

Our pursuit of these objectives raises two of the most important questions which face the British people today:

- First, can anything really be done about unemployment? Or is it 'one of the great unsolved mysteries of our time'?
- Secondly – a vital but neglected issue – what sort of jobs do we wish to create?

Socialists cannot ignore the second question for the sort of work that people do, whether in paid employment or outside the labour market, at home, defines what sort of society we live in. We must have more jobs. And we must think about the working lives of the future.

CAN ANYTHING BE DONE ABOUT UNEMPLOYMENT?

Given the number of people looking for jobs, the composition of their skills and training, and their location throughout the country, the level of employment will be determined by the size, composition, and regional distribution of the demand for labour. It is the determinants of that demand which form the key to creating jobs and cutting unemployment.

The demand for labour is determined by the demand for the goods and services that workers produce, and by the technology of the production process. If there is insufficient demand for British goods then British workers will be unemployed; and if the demand for British goods fails to grow at a time when rapid technological change reduces the amount of labour required to produce a good or service, then unemployment will increase. Both these factors have contributed to the growth of unemployment under the Thatcher government. The overall level of demand for British manufactures fell sharply after the Tories came to power and has still not returned to its level under the last Labour government. At the same time, productivity growth – the growth in the amount produced each hour by each worker – has meant that fewer workers were required to produce that lower output.

The Tories have used the effects of technical progress, of the impact of the new technologies, as an excuse for the high level of unemployment. They claim that Britain is entering 'a post-industrial age' dominated by information technology, and that the rise in unemployment is a temporary phase in the process of 'structural change' as the economy adjusts to the new era. This excuse just doesn't stand up to examination. Our low level of investment has ensured that the new technologies have been introduced more slowly in Britain than in any other major country. Japan, which has had consistently the highest rate of productivity growth among the Western countries, has the lowest level of unemployment, not the highest.

The new technologies would be a 'threat' to employment if our desire for more and better goods and services grew more slowly than our ability to produce them – if we were satiated, unable to consume more. It is patently daft to suggest that this is the condition of the vast majority of people in Britain today, or even of the vast majority of people in the United States. In a sensibly run economy, the new technologies are a boon, not a threat; an opportunity to liberate ourselves from much of the drudgery of present-day production and to create the material basis for a better society.

But it is not the impact of the new technologies which is such a 'mystery' for Margaret Thatcher. Such temporary hiccups may be explained away. The mystery is: why is unemployment persisting? Why, in 1986, after seven years of Tory policies, is the rate of increase in unemployment *accelerating*?

The Tory mystery

Margaret Thatcher finds unemployment a mystery because the central point in Tory monetarist philosophy is that the operation of free markets will *automatically* adjust the level of demand to the number of workers available. Unemployment must be due to some inhibition upon the market mechanism, some institutional rigidities which are preventing the market from doing its job. But after seven years of Tory policies designed to enhance the power of the market, why, then, is unemployment still rising? A new excuse had to be found. The answer must be that the market is failing because workers are 'pricing themselves out of a job'. Cutting the wages of those in work, and the benefits of those out of work, will solve the problem.

'Pricing yourself out of a job'

Tories are usually rather vague as to what 'pricing yourself out of a job' actually means and just how 'pricing yourself in' might work. So it is worth examining this piece of propaganda at some length.

At first sight the idea seems rather obvious. If you charge too much for your services then any prospective employer would hire someone else instead. That, of course, would not affect the overall level of employment. In this case it's not possible for everyone to price themselves out of a job at the same time! But suppose *everyone* charges 'too much' for their services and refuses to accept less (say, for reasons of union solidarity), or it is illegal for the employer to pay less (wages may be fixed by wages councils or by minimum wage legislation). Since the goods which the workers would produce will be more expensive than they might otherwise have been, then it might be thought that this would mean less being bought and so fewer workers being employed. But this is not so. For although the goods are more expensive, *incomes*, and hence the demand for goods, are higher too, in roughly the same proportion – so there is no reason why unemployment should rise.

However, Nigel Lawson suggests a different 'pricing out' argument. He claims that high wages will lead businessmen to replace workers with machines. So, if unemployment is high, wages should be cut to encourage employers to adopt labour-intensive methods of production. This is the rationale behind Lawson's famous statement that he sees the future of Britain as being 'not a low-tech, but a no-tech' society. Leaving aside the craven surrender of Britain's future implicit in Lawson's position, it is evident that his argument has no bearing at all on Britain's unemployment problem. If machines were being substituted for workers then we would expect the rise in unemployment to have been accompanied by an upswing in investment. As we have seen, the opposite has been the case.

The only sense that can be made of the 'pricing out' argument is that high costs will bring high prices, leading consumers to buy goods abroad, reducing the demand for British goods and causing unemployment here at home. Obviously, costs of production affect our ability to sell in competitive markets. But a full appraisal of the influence of international competitiveness on employment requires discussion of all the factors, not just wages, which affect the pattern of international trade. That is a vital topic to which I will return in the next chapter (see pp. 68–73). For the moment I will concentrate on the role of wages.

The influence of wages on costs depends on the level of wages and the productivity of labour. So we can try to compete either by cutting wages, or by increasing productivity. Cutting wages in Nigel Lawson's 'no-tech society' is a path to disaster. It would mean trying to compete with Third World wage levels, and would impose an intolerable fall in living standards on the British people. The alternative is to raise the rate of productivity growth, and to relate pay increases to that rate of productivity growth, so that competitiveness is maintained and even enhanced. The future of Britain must be found in a sustained rate of technical progress, as the fruits of the new technologies are applied to production. It cannot lie in the direction of Lawson's wage-cutting.

In fact, this Tory slogan of workers 'pricing themselves out of jobs' is a fine example of the old ploy of 'blame the victim'. If people are unemployed it must be *their fault*. It is a sleazy attempt to shift the blame for the government's own wastrel incompetence on to the victims of its policies. It will be treated by the people of this country with the contempt it so richly deserves.

The role of government

The story that market forces automatically ensure that full employment is maintained and that resources are allocated efficiently is a fairy tale, told in the abstract, theoretical world of Western academic economists. It has been seized upon by reactionary politicians wishing to lend spurious respectability to their indifference to economic misery and waste. The mirror image of this fairy tale, which is told in the East, is that the economy will only operate efficiently if *all* economic life is controlled and directed by means of a central plan. Another bunch of reactionaries have used this story to justify *their* political ambitions. History demonstrates with startling clarity for those with eyes to see that attempts to impose either of these fairy tales on the real world prevents us all from living happily ever after. Economic development and social progress have always flowed from a potent mix of economic management and personal freedom.

The framework within which economic life proceeds must be substantially determined by government – there are no automatic market forces out there to which responsibility can be abdicated. But the market is potentially a powerful force for good. It can be a remarkable co-ordinating mechanism. Competitive markets can stimulate innovation and productive efficiency, and provide an economic environment in which individuals can experiment, can pursue their own economic ideas. The market is a good servant.

But the market is a bad master. In many areas, such as health or education, private market calculations are not efficient for the society as a whole. Monopolies, whether public or private, distort the operations of the market. The market is a brutally inefficient mechanism for developing the full potential of those who are weak or disadvantaged or discriminated against, or who have simply not had the opportunity to develop their talents. Markets are often unstable, exaggerating weaknesses and strengths, and prone to speculative excess. And the market is incapable of ensuring that the size and composition of investment, whether in machines, or in people, or in research and development, are sufficient to maintain employment today, or provide for growing employment in the future.

If the economy is to operate efficiently the government must do, at the very least, what the market does not. It must take action to determine the overall level and rate of growth of demand for British goods, and so determine the number of jobs on offer. It must take action to affect the level and composition of investment – whether that investment is in machines, in R & D, or in education and training – and so affect the level of employment in the future. It must create the opportunities for all to develop their talents to the full. It must take action to plan change, to avoid the personal pain and economic inefficiency of the disruptive convulsions which the market inflicts on a rapidly changing society.

But the government must not pretend that it can do everything. Indeed, it should not do everything. Not only does the government not have the necessary information and expertise to manage large components of the economy, but also it would be an affront to the people who work in industry to suggest that someone in Whitehall should direct their lives. Why should they co-operate if their views are not taken into account and their judgement not respected? Yet it is just that co-operation, just that participation, on which the social consensus which is the prerequisite of economic success must be built.

There is no simple answer to the appropriate balance between the respective roles in the economy of the government and of individual initiative and enterprise. There must be government action to ensure that the economy operates efficiently; arbitrary market power must be curbed or eliminated; people must be able to participate in the decisions which affect their lives. No society has achieved the ideal balance, and even if it had, what is ideal in one period of history may well be far from ideal in another. An essential strength of democratic socialists is that at all times we have a clear view of the direction in which the balance must move, and in which we must keep it moving.

A fundamental economic task of government is the elimination of unemployment. The first government to accept this responsibility was Winston Churchill's coalition government during the Second World War. The opening sentence of the famous White Paper on Employment published in 1944 declared that 'the Government accept as one of their primary aims and responsibilities the maintenance of a high and stable level of employment after the War'. The Thatcher government was the first post-war administration to repudiate that commitment.

Action for jobs

The government can affect the level of demand for British goods and services, and hence the level of employment, both directly and indirectly. Public investment in roads, bridges and the railways, or in the health service or community care, will increase employment directly. Government transfers, such as the payment of pensions or a reduction in taxes, indirectly affect the level of demand by putting more spending money in peoples' pockets. Nor is that the end of the story. In so far as a new employee in the public sector, or a new construction worker, or the recipient of a higher pension or a tax cut, spends his or her new income on British goods and services then that will create more jobs too. The people who get those jobs will in turn create yet more by their increased expenditure, and so on. This process will go on creating jobs in the UK – but not indefinitely, because some of the money will be saved not spent, some will be absorbed by taxation, and some of the money will be spent on imports, creating jobs overseas rather than in Britain.

There have been numerous careful studies as to which of the direct and indirect methods of increasing demand is the most efficient in creating jobs. The most recent of these is by the House of Commons Select Committee on Employment, a committee with a built-in Conservative majority. *All* the studies find that it costs far less to create jobs by public investment than by cutting personal taxes. The differences in cost are dramatic. The Select Committee reports that it costs between £16,000 and £26,000 to create a job by increased public investment and about £47,000 to create a job by tax cuts. Special employment measures such as the Community Programme are the cheapest of all, costing £3,000 to £4,000 per person once account has been taken of government savings on the dole and social security payments.

The reasons for the differences are not hard to work out. Whereas public investment creates jobs directly in industries such as building which are highly labour-intensive, the increase in personal income which accrues from tax cuts is partly saved and partly spent on imports. Special employment measures require little expenditure other than the payments to participants and the cost of administration. However, they are far from satisfactory. As run by the Tory government they neither provide truly constructive training, nor produce output of value.

Margaret Thatcher's obsession with personal tax cuts is easy to understand. The fact that tax cuts don't create jobs pales into insignificance beside her hatred of the public sector, her desire to emulate Ronald Reagan, and her view that 'the taxpayer' should be relieved of the burden of welfare, as though people seeking pensions or schools or health care were not also taxpayers. Since 1979 the Tory government has cut higher rate income tax, investment income surcharge, capital gains tax and capital transfer tax. The benefits of these tax cuts have gone entirely to the best-off 3–5 per cent of the population. The greatest benefit from the cuts in higher rate income tax (about £2,000 million per year) has gone to the top 5 per cent. The entire benefit from the abolition of investment income surcharge (worth £875 million per year) has gone to the richest 1 per cent. Mrs Thatcher's total give-away to the well-off amounts to £3,600 million a year; and after this she complains that the taxes paid by the average and lower-paid worker are too high!

The Labour Party does not believe, as the Tories do, that the unemployed are to blame for their plight. It has been the quite extraordinary blend of incompetence and indifference displayed by this Tory government which is to blame. Now the task is to cut unemployment. That is the central commitment of my party and it will be the central activity of the Labour government.

Labour's employment programme

The next Labour government will implement a three-part economic programme for employment:

- First, there will be a two-year emergency programme, the objective of which is to reduce registered unemployment by 1 million.
- Secondly, and simultaneously, there will be a five-year Medium Term Employment Strategy, the objective of which is to lay the foundations for steadily expanding employment beyond the two-year emergency programme.
- Thirdly, from the outset the Labour government will establish a ten-year Economic Planning Perspective, planning the long-term structural development of the economy, and of employment, to ensure that employment is sustained in the future.

These three programmes form an interdependent and coherent strategy for economic recovery in Britain.

The first, crucial, task will be to implement the emergency jobs programme. Our plan to reduce unemployment by 1 million in our first two years in office is based on a carefully costed balance of public investment in the roads and in house-building, in the railways and other public construction; an expansion of employment in the caring services, most of which have seen their staff cut to levels which have severely inhibited their efforts to provide effective aid to the community, and a complete reconstruction and extension of special employment schemes, to ensure that the substantive two-year training and education programmes are geared to the requirements of the Medium Term Employment Strategy. The local authorities, most of which have been forced by the Tories to postpone essential building work and vital repairs, and to decimate basic community services, will play a major part in the emergency programme.

This programme will cost about £6,000 million in the first year – not so much more than the amount that Nigel Lawson tells us he wants to give away in tax cuts. Lawson's commitment in his 1986 budget speech to cut the standard rate of income tax to 25 pence in the pound would have a net cost of well over £4,000 million.

The jobs programme will receive a helpful boost from Labour's anti-poverty programme, the other emergency programme which we will introduce immediately on taking office. This programme is self-financing. It involves recouping the £3,600 million per year in tax cuts which the richest members of our society have received from the Tories, and using that money to help the poorest members of our society whom the Tories have penalized, in particular the pensioners. Since the poor spend more on British goods than do the rich, the transfer of income from rich to poor will help to create jobs.

But can we afford our emergency programme?

Taken literally, the familiar Tory whine that we 'can't afford' to spend money to cut unemployment is total nonsense. What do we have to do without? When workers and machines are lying idle, setting them to work imposes no direct real cost on the economy. A hospital built by previously unemployed bricklayers does not cut factory building. A newly employed nurse does not reduce the number of available bank clerks. Britain is not in the position of a household in which repainting the house means no money for a holiday. It's more like a family firm in which the factory has been allowed to deteriorate. But the family would rather let the works decay and fall into ruin than borrow some money from the bank, hire local builders and renew machinery, so restoring the business, creating jobs in the local building trade and maintaining factory employment in the future.

There are, of course, some obvious constraints on this process for our imaginary household. There has, for instance, to be the will to set about the reconstruction, and a willingness to borrow to set the process going.

There are, similarly, constraints on our economy, and we have to face up to them, analyse them, and then overcome them, rather than throwing our hands up and saying nothing can be done.

47

It is the very nature of an emergency programme that some of the jobs created in the first two years will be temporary. Those who enter the new two-year training programme will need jobs at the end of the programme. That is why the other two components of our strategy are important. We must look beyond the emergency programme to the creation of jobs in an expanding economy. The Medium Term Employment Strategy is a strategy for industrial recovery, for the sustainable expansion of output of goods and services, and for the development of new patterns of work and employment.

The Employment Strategy is about jobs; the Economic Planning Perspective is about industrial efficiency. The former is dependent on the latter. Only if our industry is efficient, by which I mean able to recapture the markets both at home and abroad that it has lost, will there be a sufficient demand for British goods to maintain British employment.

Only a modern, technologically sophisticated industry is capable of capturing markets in today's competitive world. In such an industry fewer people will be required to produce any given level of output. For this reason I do not expect, even when we have successfully recaptured the markets that the Tories have lost, that there will be a major increase in employment in our manufacturing industry. But the recovery of our manufacturing industry is the prerequisite of growing employment in other sectors of the economy. For selling manufactures is how we pay our way in the world. Unless we can pay our way in the world we will be plagued by balance-of-payments crises, financial crises, and inflation, and the jobs programme will grind to a halt.

Our three-part programme is designed to remove the constraints which limit employment in Britain – once, that is, the major constraint, the Tory government, is removed. The most important constraint is that of the balance of payments, but other constraints associated with finance and inflation have to be dealt with too. Indeed, all these limitations on our action are interlinked. We must overcome them in a way that is acceptable and commands widespread support.

The balance of payments

Given the severely weakened state of British industry, any major expansion of employment will suck imports into the British economy, thus creating new jobs abroad but not at home. The Tories have been able to cover the deficit created by the impact of their policies on manufacturing competitiveness by exporting oil. As the oil runs down, this option runs out. In the future, economic expansion is likely to precipitate a severe deterioration of the balance of payments, leading to a balance-of-payments deficit. Although a deficit can be covered in the short run by borrowing from abroad (that, after all, is what Ronald Reagan has done) in the long run it will lead to the sort of financial crisis that was a familiar aspect of Britain's economy in the fifties and sixties. This is why the traditional remedy for unemployment, an expansion of government investment, is not by itself a sufficient basis for a resilient growth of employment in the long term. Traditional Keynesianism is just not enough.

An effective employment strategy must have at its core an industrial policy. We must create a modern, competitive industry. Unless we can recapture markets at home and abroad we will be faced with two options. Either we will grow more and more slowly relative to our major competitors so that we do not import too much from them, thus allowing ourselves to become relatively impoverished, unable to afford the imports associated with higher levels of income; or, alternatively, we could cut ourselves off from the world economy, isolate ourselves in a cocoon of backwardness, unable to compete. Neither of these options is acceptable to the Labour Party, and we do not believe that either would be acceptable to the British people.

Labour's objective is to build a competitive, innovative, modern industrial sector in Britain. Industrial policy must be at the very core of our employment programme. Here long-term and short-term policy objectives merge in their policy prescriptions. If employment growth is to be sustained in the long term, manufacturing industry must be strong enough and competitive

49

enough to pay for the imports we need. That means there must be a major increase in investment – investment in modern industrial capacity, in education and training, and in research. This increase in investment will also increase employment in the short term. So a carefully structured investment programme will both help to provide the immediate upsurge in employment that we desperately need, and provide the means to sustain that growth of employment in the longer term.

However, an investment programme on the scale required will itself impose severe strains on the balance of payments. Not only do we need to import some of the very latest machines, but newly employed workers will tend to buy their share of imported consumer goods. Also, the severe loss of markets that we have suffered at home and abroad is a powerful disincentive to investment. These problems raise some difficult questions concerning trade policy both at the level of the individual industry and at the overall, economy-wide level (including the question of exchange rate policy). I will examine these questions in chapters 5 and 7 respectively. Suffice it to say here that the balance-of-payments constraint on the growth of employment cannot be treated, as has typically been the case in the past, solely as a problem of overall, macroeconomic policy. Quite the contrary. It must be treated as a problem of microeconomic, industrial policy, and macroeconomic policy must be suited to its needs.

Balance-of-payments difficulties are closely linked to domestic financial problems and to the rate of inflation. Problems with the pound lead to loss of confidence in the government's financial strategy and a falling pound pushes up the inflation rate. Both loss of financial confidence and inflation can limit the scope of the government's action on jobs.

Sound money

The government's ability to finance the sort of expenditure programme which is required to sustain the first two parts of Labour's three-part strategy for jobs is inhibited by the need to pursue a financial policy which is perceived to be 'sound'. If financial confidence is lost the consequent difficulties will severely limit the jobs programme.

The Tories have linked 'sound money' to the public sector borrowing requirement. They have made such a fetish out of the PSBR that they have convinced the financial community that it is the key indicator by which the wisdom of any policy is to be judged. Now even the Tories are wriggling around in the attempt to escape the cage created by their own folly.

The public sector borrowing requirement measures the differences between the flow of receipts and the flow of expenditure into and out of the public sector. Concentrating on the difference between receipts and expenditure focuses attention on the amount which the government must borrow (assuming expenditure greater than receipts). This was thought to have some merit when it used to be claimed that government borrowing 'crowded out' private borrowing, so that public expenditure was at the expense of private investment. This argument was common in the thirties and in the early years of the Thatcher government. In an underemployed economy it is as nonsensical as the 'can't afford it' slogan. By setting unemployed resources to work, government expenditure increases incomes *and* saving.

A fatal weakness of the PSBR as a measure of the government's impact on the economy is that it makes no distinction between current transactions (receiving taxes and paying pensions) and capital transactions (receiving money from the sale of a redundant aircraft carrier and buying some buildings). The failure to distinguish between current and capital transactions is a failure to distinguish between activities which use resources for consumption or investment and those which do not use resources, but involve simply a transfer of ownership of existing assets. This can have serious consequences. Thus we have the extraordinary sight of a government selling off British assets and using the receipts for tax cuts. This is rather like a company selling off its machinery and paying out the receipts in dividends to the shareholders. This is a process which cannot go on for long; eventually there are no more pay-outs and the shareholders' stock is worth nothing – it has become a claim on non-existent assets.

The analogy is not quite perfect because selling off assets to the private sector allows production to continue, in principle at least, so that the government could always increase taxation on the newly privatized companies and their employees to replace and even exceed the revenues it formerly received when they were nationalized. That is to say, it could privatize to cut taxes and then raise taxes in the future! This is what the City now calls 'sound finance'.

The need to maintain 'sound money', in other words the need to maintain the PSBR at a level of which the City approves, in so far as it arises at all, arises because the City *believes* the statistic to be important. The fact that something is generally believed, that each financier believes his fellow financiers will act in a particular way, makes the constraint of the PSBR a self-fulfilling prophecy. It is the level of the PSBR that comes to matter – not employment, or production, or exports or the real economy.

Since we unfortunately cannot wish away the fevered imagination of our financial sector, we must educate the City out of the PSBR nonsense. After all, no other country has a PSBR; why should we? While recognizing that rational argument may be in vain, we will present our expenditure policies in new and far more accurate ways. First, current expenditure will be measured in terms of the public sector financial deficit (which includes only current transactions and leaves out capital transactions, and so really does measure the government's impact on resource utilization in the economy). Second, the capital transactions of the government will be itemized in a public sector balance sheet. These are more than mere statistical reforms. They introduce sound accounting practice which is not present at the moment.

The enhancement of the productive capacity and competitiveness of the British economy is not just a government objective; it must also be the prime objective of the financial community if confidence in the financial system is to be retained. The customary distinction between the fate of the City on the one hand and the separate fate of industry on the other is a delusion. The financial community can only prosper in the long run if the real economy prospers. To that end the Labour government will pursue a common-sense financial policy, expressed in terms of indicators with real economic meaning, and which supports the expansion of industry. We will not sacrifice production, and hence employment, on an altar of financial fetishism. We will borrow to produce more and to sell more.

Inflation

Any major upsurge in inflation which is not obviously due to events abroad, such as a rise in commodity prices, will pose a threat to our jobs programme. This is not because there is a mechanical causal link between inflation and unemployment. That idea has been consistently refuted by events. The notion that unemployment should be kept high to keep inflation low is therefore not only appallingly wasteful, but wrong. Yet it is undoubtedly true that nothing will destroy the prospect of growing employment more rapidly and more comprehensively than an upsurge in inflation. The reason for this is two-fold.

First, if inflation is higher in Britain than it is abroad, foreign goods become relatively cheap and rising incomes provide the British with the wherewithal to buy foreign goods. Thus inflation exacerbates the balance-of-payments constraint. A deterioration in the balance of payments tends to lead to a fall in the value of the pound which pushes up the cost of imported materials and causes inflation to accelerate. A vicious circle is created. Second, inflation itself discredits an economic policy, destroys the consensus which an effective policy requires. High rates of inflation have become symbolic of failure in economic management. Failure is infectious and, once contracted, is difficult to eradicate.

To attack inflation we must know what causes it. Clearly, inflation can be imported, either because of price rises overseas, or because the exchange rate falls significantly for an extended period and pushes up import prices in sterling terms. Rising import prices both push up costs directly and lead to increases in money wages as workers seek to protect their living standards. The rate of inflation can also be lowered by import prices falling, as happened in the first half of 1986 as oil prices and other commodity prices fell.

Inflation may also be generated within the economy. Money wages are set by collective bargaining. Prices (and hence profits) are set by corporate management as a mark-up on costs. In striking a bargain, and in fixing prices, workers and management are attempting to obtain an amount of money which has a particular real purchasing power. Workers are interested in what they can buy with a week's wages. If real purchasing power, real wages, are cut by corporate price rises then workers will demand pay rises to maintain their standard of living. If pay rises cut into profits firms will push up prices. Each party to the bargaining, workers and management, typically has some level of real income that it is aiming for, and for which it would be willing to settle.

If the economy is growing steadily and output and sales per worker are rising, increases in money wages do not affect costs too much and prices rise less rapidly than wages. The spending power of wages rises and so do profits. The harmony of those conditions is, however, broken if output stagnates or even declines and workers' efforts to maintain their standard of living cut into the profit targets that companies are trying to achieve. Companies then promptly raise prices, cutting the value of wages. The workers demand higher money wages to restore living standards. This raises costs, so prices are put up again, so wages are raised again, inflation spirals on and on. Rising import prices or increased taxes, such as increases in VAT, will also set this spiral off, as we saw after the oil price increases in 1973 and 1979, and after the Tory VAT increases in 1979.

The spiral will continue so long as neither workers nor companies obtain levels of real income with which they are satisfied. Inflation can be cut by increasing output so that all demands are satisfied; by forcing either workers to accept lower real wages or firms to accept lower real profits; or by reaching a political agreement as to how the national product is to be distributed and used.

So, contrary to the Tory belief that cutting output and employment reduces inflation, in current circumstances the opposite is true. Increasing output, and thus increasing productivity, is the way to remove inflationary pressures.

However, increasing output takes time, and it is vital that neither external events, nor an internal struggle to obtain output that is not yet there, should create an inflationary spiral which would damage the jobs programme. It will be one of the major tasks of the Labour Party's planned National Economic Assessment to prevent such a spiral taking off. The National Economic Assessment will involve government, management and trades unions in deliberation about the distribution of national production among private consumption, social consumption (education, health, the welfare state) and investment. Gaining and maintaining a national consensus on the distribution of our national product will have clear implications for wages and profits, and it will establish a direct link between the achievement of targets in investment, output and job creation, and wages and prices. It is essential, of course, that all concerned participate in all the relevant decisions. For example, it is ridiculous to suppose that trades unions should agree to a particular scale of wage and salary share in the national product but have no say in the determination of the rate of investment and innovation. It would be equally unhelpful to suppose that companies should pursue an agreed expansionary investment policy only to see costs rise and markets disappear as inflation outstrips price rises abroad. And no-one should think that the Government could commit resources to investment or consumption without having evidence that those resources would be used for the intended purposes of strengthening production, improving services and generating jobs.

Of course, building a consensus takes time, both at the national level and at the level of the individual firm. The task of the government in this process is threefold:

- first, to establish the institutional and informational framework within which the speedy negotiation and practical operation of a consensus can take place;
- secondly, to set out its own objectives – including the central aim of reducing unemployment by 1 million in two years – and the relationship between those objectives and rewards in the private and the public sectors;
- thirdly, to protect the interests of those who are not directly represented in the Assessment, whether they are pensioners, welfare recipients, low-paid workers who are not represented in collective bargaining, the consumers of today or the consumers and workers of tomorrow.

The government would have to have manifest co-operation from all parties concerned in order to sustain full commitment to investment, consumption and expansion. We will not be deflected from our course if co-operation is not forthcoming or as full as it needs to be. But clearly we will then have to proceed more slowly, and that cannot be to anyone's advantage.

The state to which the British economy has been reduced by Thatcherism is such as to constitute a national emergency. That is why the Labour Party seeks to implement its policies for national reconstruction by building a national consensus. The National Economic Assessment, a review of where we stand, what we need to do and how we need to do it, is designed to help develop that consensus. By definition, a consensus can be worked for, but it cannot be imposed. In a democracy, if people or organizations are unwilling to participate, and unwilling to agree in an arrangement that is necessarily voluntary, then a democratic government cannot sensibly take draconian powers of enforcement. It is, however, clear that a government that cannot plan the supply and use of resources with the co-operation and involvement of other parties must, nevertheless, plan those resources anyway. It cannot and must not opt out of that responsibility. But it must then discharge the duty without the advantages which consensus confers and, equally, without the obligations that consensus imposes. In short, if consensus and its assistance are not available from other participants, then considerate responses from government are not justifiable and will not be forthcoming. That is not governmental vanity or vindictiveness. It is reality.

I will have more to say about building a consensus around our strategy for Britain's recovery when I deal in chapters 5 and 7 with the issue of just how we get industry moving. But in our drive to modernize Britain, we must also consider what sort of society we want to live in. Production is not an end in itself, but the means of providing the material foundations of a better society. Part of that better society involves the process of production itself. We must be concerned with *how* things are produced and *by whom* they are produced, as well as how much is produced and at what cost. Indeed, all these elements are interrelated. The efficiency of production is determined by people, not by machines. That is why we must address the question raised at the beginning of this chapter, what sort of jobs do we want to create?

WHAT SORT OF JOBS?

The traditional definition of full employment was the provision of a job for every *man* who wanted one, where a job is defined as 40 hours a week, 47 or 48 weeks a year, for around 45 years of life. This is a definition derived from the society of the nineteenth century (the only real, hard-won concession to the twentieth century being a few extra years at school, a couple of extra weeks' holiday and a retirement pension). It is an inappropriate and inefficient characterization of what full employment should mean for Britain today.

The desperate desire of millions of people to get a job and the ever-present fear of unemployment in Mrs Thatcher's Britain might give the impression that consideration of what sort of jobs we want to create is a luxury we cannot afford. Providing jobs with traditional employment patterns of 40 hours a week for 45 years is far better than there being no jobs at all. But it should be noted that this pattern of employment is profoundly inefficient in (at least) four ways: first, it excludes from full participation in production many workers (particularly, but not exclusively, women) who cannot commit themselves to the traditional pattern of paid employment because they have personal and social responsibilities which demand that they work in the home; secondly, it fails to relate the duration of working life either to the nature of the job or to the nature of the individual; thirdly, it does not allow for the systematic training and retraining, for the commitment of time to the regular reorganization of working life, which is a necessary feature of a modern technological society; fourthly, it fails to take account of the impact on efficiency and employment of a labour force which is 'stretched' by overtime working.

Flexibility in the daily, yearly and lifetime distribution of time among paid employment, work outside paid employment, education and training, and leisure, would not only enhance the quality of life, but would also be more efficient than the rigid employment structure which is typical today.

We waste the skills of women whose opportunities are constrained because society does not make adequate provision for the particular needs of those with babies or young children. Instead of adapting patterns of work and of career development to fit their needs, they are too often forced into ill-paid employment with no opportunities for development, because those jobs are the only part-time jobs available, or because the break from work involved in caring for young children restricts them permanently to the lower rungs of the career ladder.

Our attitude to retirement is also far too rigid. People today are fearful of early retirement because all too often it means a sharp fall in living standards. Yet in many occupations, particularly the more arduous, early retirement should be encouraged by making the prospect far more attractive, both in terms of material provision and preparation and in the possibilities available for developing other productive and satisfying activities.

And if we are to maintain and enhance the abilities of our labour force, then education and training must not be something which is provided in a single burst in the teens and twenties. They must be lifelong activities to which all have regular access.

We should remember that the total number of people seeking employment is affected not only by the demand for labour (in a buoyant labour market people who in a slump had not thought it worthwhile to look for a job will try to find work) but also by what sort of jobs and what kind of conditions of employment are available. This is another important reason why more flexible working conditions are more efficient.

Clearly the long-term development of material prosperity should change the pattern and content of work and leisure. But there are measures related to the nature of employment which can and should be taken *now* to make our economy more efficient. Greater flexibility in conditions of employment, protection and support for those who seek more flexible arrangements, and a more imaginative approach to retirement – these are things which can be legislated for and introduced gradually *now*, and which would improve the lives of many people and make the economy more efficient for generations to come.

Ultimately our success in building a better, more equal, more fulfilling and freer society in Britain will depend upon our success in solving Britain's industrial problems. Without an efficient, growing economy all our plans for a better society will be ground down by the bitter forces of recession. We must build an efficient industry for a better society.

Creating Jobs

INDUSTRIAL POLICY

My persistent argument is that if we are to create jobs we must build an efficient, competitive industry. There may be two reactions to this: it might appear obvious to some, and para-doxical to others. The paradox may seem to derive from the fact that efficiency typically means less workers for a given output. So if output stayed the same, employment would fall.

However, as I have already argued above, if efficiency does not increase, then markets will be lost at home and abroad. The resulting squeeze on the balance of payments (and rise in the rate of inflation) will force the government to depress the rate of growth of the economy. The result will be a lower level of invest-ment, less training, less R & D, further loss of markets, and yet further loss of jobs.

If industry is efficient, is capturing markets at home and abroad, then pressure is taken off the balance of payments and off the rate of inflation. The rate of growth which the economy can sustain is therefore higher. Investment, research and train-ing can all proceed at a higher rate. The result will not neces-sarily be many more jobs in the export industries, or even in those industries which compete with imports. After all, greater efficiency does mean more output from the same number of workers. But the enhanced competitiveness is absolutely neces-sary if output and employment are to be expanded in other sectors of the economy faster than they otherwise could be, whether these involve private or public services, construction or transportation.

Of course, it isn't just industry which competes for markets around the world. Services are very important too. But I believe that the key to the future of the British economy is to be found specifically in the future of our manufacturing industry. It is upon the development of a truly competitive manufacturing industry that prospects for employment depend.

60

4
Why Manufacturing?

I am at a loss to understand the selective importance attached by the opposition and some Tories to the manufacturing sector.

Nigel Lawson, 1984

Nigel Lawson's gentle puzzlement turned to petulant abuse in the autumn of 1985 when the House of Lords Select Committee on Overseas Trade presented a carefully argued case for the particular importance of manufacturing industry. Even before the report was published Nigel Lawson dismissed it as 'a mixture of special pleading dressed up as analysis and assertion masquerading as evidence'. Leon Brittan, who was then Secretary of State for Trade and Industry, declared that 'this report needs to be set in perspective if we are not to get a totally biased and misleading view of the performance and prospects of our economy'. He did not reveal what that 'perspective' might be.

Harsh words. Lord Aldington, a former Chairman of the Conservative party who was the Chairman of the House of Lords Committee, could only comment, in a somewhat bemused manner: 'The most dispiriting thing is Lawson's refusal to accept there is an urgent situation. Manifestly the Chancellor and Leon Brittan have not got the point.'

The arguments which had so neatly exposed the emptiness of Nigel Lawson's economic thinking, and which stung him into such a revealing display, are worth quoting in full.

> Unless the climate is changed so that the manufacturing base is
> enlarged and steps are taken to ensure that import penetration is
> combatted and that manufactured exports are stimulated, as the
> oil revenues diminish the country will experience adverse effects
> which will worsen with time. These will include:
>
> (i) a contraction of manufacturing to the point where the
> successful continuation of much of manufacturing activity is put
> at risk;
>
> (ii) an irreplaceable loss of GDP;
>
> (iii) an adverse balance of payments of such proportion that
> severely deflationary measures will be needed;
>
> (iv) lower tax revenues for public spending on welfare,
> defence and other areas;
>
> (v) higher unemployment, with little prospect of reducing it;
> and
>
> (vi) the economy stagnating and inflation rising, driven up by
> a falling exchange rate.
>
> The Committee take the view that, together, these prospects
> constitute a grave threat to the standard of living of the British
> people. Failure to recognise these dangers now could have a de-
> vastating effect on the future economic and political stability of
> the nation. The situation in which we find ourselves is not self-
> correcting: things will not come right of their own accord. Urgent
> action is required, not only by government but by everyone.

A few pages further on in their Report, the House of Lords
Committee commented:

> ... the paramountcy of manufacturing has not been recognised
> [by the Government] in the formation of policies, with the result
> that policies – or the avowed lack of policies – have actually been
> inimical to manufacturing ... governments of whatever political
> persuasion should strive for faster growth of manufacturing and
> in setting their macro-economic policy should be mindful of
> industry's needs. (pp. 60–1)

Nigel Lawson's pique at the demonstration that the Government's economic policy has no clothes is not difficult to understand. He could scarcely make public contrition. Yet his failure to act, the failure of Margaret Thatcher's government to act, is beyond comprehension. For the Committee's chilling conclusion concerning the consequence of Tory policy for 'the future economic and political stability of the nation' is confirmed by every serious observer of the British economy, of whatever political persuasion.

The British Association of Chambers of Commerce has argued that the government has 'no convincing answer' as to what will happen to the economy as North Sea oil declines.

The CBI, although it never staged the 'bare-knuckle fight' with the Tory government over the destruction of manufacturing industry which was threatened by its Director-General in 1981, has repeatedly called for a change of direction.

The Invisible Exports Council declares that it does not regard the growth of the service industries 'as being to a major extent a substitute for decline in general industrial activity'.

The point that all these commentators are making is that there can be no prospect of long-term prosperity for the British economy without a major recovery of our manufacturing industry. Indeed, the situation is even worse than this. Unless there is a major recovery of our manufacturing industry *within the next five to ten years*, the average standard of living in Britain will fall. It does not require a morbid turn of mind to imagine the effect on our society of a persistently falling, or even a static, standard of living. That is why the years of neglect and dismissal of the importance of manufacturing industry by the Conservative government have been so damaging.

The belief that the development and redevelopment of manufacturing industry are crucial to our future does not derive from sentimentality or from delusions of economic grandeur. The old workshop of the world where outdated goods were made on museum-piece machines by antique methods closed a long time ago and it isn't going to re-open. It comes from the practical recognition of the fact of life that as the oil revenues and production begin to fall we must make and sell extra goods of equivalent value if we are to hope to maintain our current levels of output, employment and living standards, let alone start to cut the dole queues.

TRADE IN MANUFACTURES

International trade plays a vital role in the British economy. Thirty-four pence out of every pound we spend goes on imports. Those imports have to be paid for by export earnings. It is possible to pay out more than we earn for a few years and cover the difference by borrowing from foreign governments or foreign banks. But borrowing to cover deficits can only go on for a limited number of years. Unless it produces evidence of money well spent in the form of higher and better production, sales and income, those who have lent the wherewithal to pay import bills eventually baulk at the size of the borrowing and begin to assert the power of creditors to dictate economic policies that will serve their purpose of recovering their money, regardless of what are the best interests of the British people. To avoid that happening as the oil runs out we must either sell more exports or buy fewer imports.

Our export earnings are derived from sales of goods and services, and from the balance of the interest and dividend payments flowing into the country from our investments abroad and out of the country from foreigners' investments here. The goods we sell have, until recently, been predominantly manufactures. Now we also sell oil. The services we sell include shipping, tourism, banking and insurance, and education.

Even today, after seven difficult years for our manufacturing industry, the majority of our export earnings come from the sale of manufactures. Of our earnings from the sale of goods and services, about 17 per cent derives from the sale of fuels, about 23 per cent from services, and about 51 per cent from the sale of manufactures. The remaining 9 per cent is made up of food, drink and tobacco, and basic materials.

The difference in scale between trade in manufactures and trade in services is an indication of the vital role of manufactured goods. Indeed, the size of earnings from the sale of manufactures relative to that of earnings from services has not changed significantly in the past 20 years. What has changed, quite dramatically, are the individual trade balances in manufactures, services, and fuels. Figure 1 tells us an extraordinary story. (In this figure, the annual net returns of interest, dividends

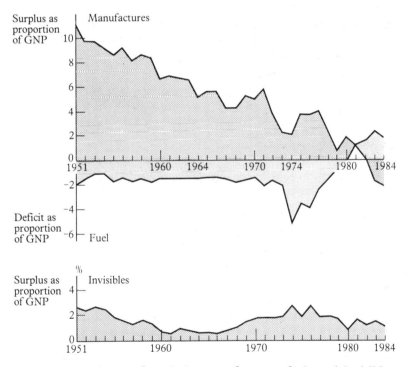

Figure 1 Balance of trade in manufactures, fuels and invisibles, expressed as a proportion of GNP, UK 1951–84.
Source: Annual Abstract of Statistics.

and profits from abroad are added to services to give total 'invisible' incomes.)

In the early fifties the surplus on our trade in manufactures was worth more than 10 per cent of our gross national product. It has declined almost continuously since then, although the rate of decline was slowed significantly by the Labour governments in the sixties and seventies. In 1982, manufactured trade slipped into deficit, and it has stayed there ever since. Trade in services has led a far less eventful life. The surplus on invisibles has hovered between 1 per cent and 2 per cent of gross national product, declining toward the bottom end of the range in recent years, primarily because of the fall in revenue earned from shipping. If our trade in services has a new relative significance it is because of the fall in the manufactured trade balance, not a rise in the 'invisible' balance.

Trade in fuels also followed a predictable pattern from the fifties to the oil crisis of 1973. Our deficit on fuels was always worth about 2 per cent of gross national product. In 1973, when the oil price rose, the deficit worsened suddenly to 5 per cent of gross national product. But then, as North Sea oil came on stream, the deficit was transformed rapidly into a surplus – just in time for Margaret Thatcher's government to enjoy the luxury of being able to ignore the plight of manufacturing by hiding behind the oil revenues.

The overall picture, then, is one of a massive surplus on trade in manufactures (which was used to pay for the deficit on imported raw materials and foodstuffs which is not shown in figure 1) which has been steadily eroded, a persistent surplus on trade in services which shows no signs of growing significantly and a persistent deficit on fuels which is enjoying a brief excursion into glorious surplus, and will all too soon return to deficit again.

Figure 1 does not tell the full story, however. Since on average, over a period of years, we are obliged by commercial reality to pay our way in the world, all the surpluses and deficits must balance out. If trade in food and materials had been added to the diagram it would have provided the large deficit which offset the large manufacturing surplus of the sixties. In recent years that deficit has been reduced somewhat. To a considerable extent this is due to the dramatic improvement in the efficiency of British agriculture derived from comprehensive government planning of agricultural development since the war. Measures have ranged from marketing boards, which stabilize demand and ensure that your pinta is delivered to your door, to comprehensive agricultural research and advisory services. The success of British agriculture, which was established well before our entry into the EEC, is an example of just how successful well-thought-out economic planning can be.

Since the trading surpluses and deficits of all the sectors of the economy must, taken together, roughly balance out, it is necessary to investigate which of them is changing because of underlying economic circumstances and which is simply adjusting to make up the balance.

The steady worsening of the manufacturing deficit has been made up of two mutually reinforcing trends. We have been persistently losing our share of world markets in manufactures, while foreign producers have been persistently capturing a larger and larger share of our markets. For example, since 1979 our share of the market for manufactured exports in the main industrial countries has fallen from 9.7 per cent to 7.6 per cent. In the same period the proportion of all manufactures sold in Britain which are imported has risen from 26.5 per cent to 33 per cent, most of them coming from the other main industrial countries. There has been a persistent, underlying tendency for manufactured imports to grow faster than manufactured exports.

In the service industries, despite the fact that in the past seven years they have suffered a loss of world market share equally as dramatic as that suffered in manufactures, imports have grown at round the same rate as exports, so that the same overall balance has been preserved.

If the trends in trade in manufactures, so evident and so

persistent, are not reversed *permanently* then they will clearly negate any upturn which may occur in the trade of the far smaller services sector. That is why the House of Lords Select Committee identified the future of manufacturing as being so crucial to our economic future. That is why Nigel Lawson's behaviour in fiddling around with petty policies to suit the City while ignoring what was happening in manufacturing has been so disgraceful. That is why the Labour Party has placed the recovery of manufacturing industry, *as measured by its perform-ance in international trade*, the only true, unambiguous measure of success, at the very core of our economic policy.

CHANGING THE BALANCE OF EXPORTS AND IMPORTS

There are three basic ways in which an imbalance between imports and exports can *in principle* be adjusted without the introduction of a major recovery programme for manufac-turing.

First, the currency can be devalued to make imports more expensive and exports cheaper. The resulting price cut in exports can help to improve trade performance. But it is far from being a complete solution to Britain's problems, because, regrettably, its effects for our country are less powerful than in many other countries, because of our dependence on imported raw materials, part-finished goods and, now, manufactured goods, including machinery. While we can boost foreign sales with a currency price cut, we also increase the costs of living and of production and so diminish the trade-promoting effects of the devaluation. Moreover, trade in manufactures is not determined solely by their price. Expensive German goods are bought by producers and consumers because they are well designed, well engineered, up-to-date, and now have a self-sustaining reputa-tion for being delivered on time and not breaking down. These 'non-price' factors have a major effect on the flows of inter-national trade, and are not easily deflected, even by falls in the exchange rate. So a devaluation is unlikely to bring permanent benefits unless all the non-price factors are improved too. Changes in the exchange rate do not have a big impact on British trade precisely because many British goods tend to be uncompetitive in 'non-price' terms.

The beneficial effects of a devaluation are also offset by the impact of the devaluation on the rate of inflation. Here the choking grip of a balance-of-payments constraint is starkly revealed in its full power. For not only is a weak balance of payments in itself a constraint on economic growth and employment, but also the fall in the exchange rate which accompanies a balance-of-payments deficit will tend to accelerate the rate of inflation at home, thus tightening the inflation constraint too. The two constraints interact upon and reinforce each other. Devaluation accelerates inflation both directly, through raising the cost of imports, and indirectly, by raising the cost of living and so leading to higher wage demands as workers attempt to avoid cuts in their living standards. This rise in prices will offset competitive advantages obtained from the devaluation and strengthen the hand of those calling for more unemployment to combat inflation.

Devaluation *can* be a successful strategy to gain competitiveness, but only if the products are right, if the boost to domestic inflation can be offset and the stimulus to sales is sustained. In the longer run, maintaining a lower rate of inflation than that of competitors can, *as long as the quality is there*, lead to a persistent desirable effect as exports gain a steady, year-on-year price advantage in foreign markets, and imports are steadily disadvantaged.

We have ample evidence that, in the case of Britain, devaluations have not, up to now, proved to be successful in turning around the *trend* decline in manufactured trade – though they did have some beneficial effect for a short time. The problem has been that they were reactions to pressing problems and not accompanied by the industrial policies which would improve the performance of manufacturing industry. They were defensive measures rather than part of an economic battle plan. Devaluation can hold ground temporarily, but it cannot, of itself, secure advance. And merely holding ground that is now so much lower than it was even seven years ago is just not enough to meet the needs of industrial survival, let alone the progress that is required.

We also have ample evidence of the devastating effect that an exchange rate moving the *wrong way* can have on manufactured trade. If the products are not right and the inflation rate is deliberately accelerated by raising VAT, then raising the exchange rate and interest rates as well is a sure recipe for disaster. The first three years of Thatcher government demonstrated only too clearly how big that disaster can be. Even now, in 1986, the high interest rate, high exchange rate policies beloved of Nigel Lawson are keeping our prices 10 per cent higher relative to those of our competitors than they were when Mrs Thatcher took office.

The second way to improve the balance of trade is to reduce the level of output and employment. The lower level of output will mean that fewer imported materials are required. The lower level of employment will mean that the incomes of many people are severely cut as they are thrown onto the dole queues, and they will no longer be able to afford to buy so many imported goods. This is a sure-fire way to eliminate a balance of payments problem. So long as he or she is willing to depress industry and impoverish the people to a sufficient degree then any fool can secure some sort of surplus on the balance of payments. A successful economic policy is one which secures a reasonable balance of trade and payments *with rising employment* and with a rate of growth that is well above the 0.9 per cent average of the Thatcher years.

Throughout the past thirty years growth in Britain has been slower than the average rate for the OECD countries – the other main industrialized countries. From 1960 to 1973 the OECD growth rate was 1.5 times higher than that of Britain (the OECD averaged 4.5 per cent per year while we managed 3.0 per cent per year). From 1973 to 1979, after the first oil shock, the OECD grew twice as fast as we did (the OECD rate was 2.7 per cent per year, Britain's rate 1.3 per cent per year). From 1979 to 1985, under Mrs Thatcher, our growth rate has sunk to significantly less than half the OECD rate of 2.1 per cent per year.

In the sixties that relatively slow rate of growth, that slow relative impoverishment of our people, was sufficient to keep the growth of imports down to a level which we could just about afford to pay for. Indeed, by the end of the sixties the Labour government had made fair strides towards at least stopping the rot in manufactured trade. In the seventies a semblance of balance could be maintained only by Britain growing far more slowly than our competitors, that is, by raising the rate of relative impoverishment.

Now, in the mid-eighties, the performance of our manufacturing industry has deteriorated so badly that we cannot sustain a decent balance even though the rate of relative impoverishment is yet higher. Unless something is done, and done rapidly, our growth rate relative to that of the rest of the world will be forced lower and lower. This has an appalling potential in itself. Given that the prospects for growth in the world economy over the next decade are generally agreed to be rather less favourable than they were in the sixties, the consequences are frightening since we will not even have as much growth in other countries to pull us along. Competitive stagnation is certainly no way to secure a trade balance. If it were, we should hold a celebration every time a factory closed.

The third way of adjusting trade flows is to intervene directly, with tariffs or quotas. These have a distinct advantage over devaluation in that direct action can yield predictable results, and tariffs and quotas can be targeted to influence trade in those sectors which are likely to bring the greatest long-term advantages to the economy. Moreover, the inflationary effect of direct measures is less severe than with a devaluation. The price rises created by a tariff, for example, can be offset by using the revenue from the tariff to cut the general rate of VAT.

71

The obvious disadvantage of this course is that other countries are likely to react against such overt measures to change the pattern of trade, and take economic reprisals against our exporters. Such a reaction is crude and self-defeating. If a vigorous growth strategy is aborted because too many imports are sucked into the economy, the cut in imports produced by that stagnation and the subsequent recession means a cut in exports for trading partners. If, instead, that vigorous growth is maintained by limiting the growth of imports to that which can be afforded, trading partners enjoy *at least* the same volume of exports, the customer economy becomes stronger and the potential for future sales greater, and the world economy as a whole grows faster, benefiting everyone.

If direct measures are used as part of an expansionary strategy they can be advantageous to all. If they are used to cut imports while not stimulating growth then they truly are beggar-my-neighbour tactics which are foolish and wrong. In the past 20 years such folly has led to the international trading system being affected by creeping protection in many countries. As protection begets protection, the results of not breaking the habit now and moving towards a system of co-operative and co-ordinated policies to promote growth and international trade are, as I shall argue in chapter 7, potentially disastrous for the whole world.

Like devaluation, tariffs and quotas will not lead to any long-term improvement in the country's trading position unless they are accompanied by an industrial policy designed to revive manufacturing industry and produce modern goods competitively. Devaluation without an industrial policy amounts to oxygen-tent economics – useful for essential resuscitation, useless for proper recovery. Quotas and tariffs which are not part of a recovery strategy can similarly give temporary respite, but not resilient strength.

The three methods of adjusting the structure of trade all point to the urgent necessity of a comprehensive recovery strategy for British manufacturing industry. There is no long-term way to adjust trade patterns without it. Failure to accept that and to operate systematically on that basis means fatalistically accepting permanent decline into slower growth, and increasingly desperate efforts to balance imports and exports by impoverishing millions. It is, of course, an extreme version of this futile strategy which is currently being imposed by the IMF upon the debtor countries of the Third World, such as Mexico. Expansion requires an industrial recovery. But industrial recovery requires expansion. No economy can be strengthened by a depression.

WHY NOT SERVICES?

The relative scales of trade in services and trade in manufactures suggest that Britain's problems cannot be resolved by switching our efforts from manufacturing to services. The service sector is not big enough to carry the burden. This is not to say that a progressive, modern banking and insurance industry, a recovery in shipping, and an improvement in our trade in education, research and development consultancy (including the burgeoning software industry) is not to be welcomed, indeed deliberately fostered. Tourism, where expertise is developing and revenue increasing, should get greater support. Service industries are not to be despised and they are not demeaning. They are simply not enough, and will never be enough to provide the foreign earnings that we need. And very little of the service sector is likely to achieve significantly greater success if it is not accompanied and led by a recovery of manufacturing.

The performance of much of the service sector is intimately linked to the performance of the manufacturing sector to which it provides many of its services. There is no prosperous country in the world whose fortunes are built on services alone. Switzerland, for example, possesses a powerful and sophisticated engineering industry, producing everything from machine tools and heavy diesel engines to the most advanced modern electronics. Swiss manufactured exports persistently grow more rapidly than Swiss manufactured imports. The Swiss financial sector thrives on the strength of its domestic economy.

It might be thought, particularly by the more prosperous ostriches in the City of London, that some services, such as international banking and insurance, have effectively detached themselves from the domestic economy, and could thrive despite the decline of industry. This is a delusion, and a very dangerous one at that. A successful financial centre requires a powerful and prosperous economy both to provide a foundation of growing domestic business and to generate a flow of savings. If the domestic economy declines, the financial sector, however international its dealings may be, will ultimately become the dependent offshoot of the financial institutions of more prosperous economies – and then slowly wither.

The strength in services was built largely upon strength in trade, and that in turn was founded upon strength in manufacturing. The strength of institutions, reputations, and expertise in those service trades has lasted longer than its foundations; but there is no guarantee that they will last forever. The names and the activities of the institutions can, and probably will, remain, but the substance can be eroded. New institutions grow elsewhere from industrial and commercial strength. Radical changes in international communications facilitate the decision-making, the transfer of resources, and the making of money in places that are physically well away from the traditional centres of banking, insurance, and commerce.

Only tourism (and teaching English as a foreign language) may be immune from the general decline. A quaint old UK with its sadly impoverished natives who are glad to provide cheap labour to wait at tables, carry bags, and provide every service the tourist requires much more cheaply than it could ever be obtained back home, would still attract visitors. But even tourism loses some of its charm when the environment is run down, the public services are shabby and the people are resentful that they have had to turn to servicing tourism because of mass unemployment.

ERROR AND EXAMPLE

Britain needs modern, expanding manufacturing industries. To say that the achievement of change on the scale and at the speed required is difficult is to grossly underestimate the size of the task, especially when account is taken of the very adverse circumstances that the next Labour government will inherit from the most destructive government of modern times. But we can succeed if we learn both from our own mistakes and from the successes of others.

The decline into deficit in manufactured trade that has occurred in the past four years is bad enough when seen as the outcome of the overall performance of the manufacturing sector. That deficit is now running at about £4,000 million a year (a turnaround from a surplus of £3,000 million in 1979). But it becomes even worse when the performance of two vital industries is examined: that of the motor-car industry, the industry that has been the mainstay of engineering and steelmaking for the past thirty years; and that of the electronics industry, the industry of the future. The deficit on the trading performance of the motor industry was £2,665 million in 1984. The deficit on trade in electronics (data processing machinery and telecommunications and audio equipment) was £1,250 million. In other words, *the deficit in just these two industries is roughly equal to the entire deficit in manufacturing*. Of course, they are not the only sectors in deficit, and other sectors are in surplus. But the deterioration of our trading performance in cars and in electronics exemplifies the ruinous deterioration of British industry under the Tories.

75

Whatever happened to our car industry?

In 1974, British Leyland, the last remaining British car producer, was about to be forced into bankruptcy. It seemed to be the end of a steady decline marked by underinvestment, bad management, persistent production problems with antiquated plant, and bad industrial relations. The company was rescued by the Labour government, using the device of the National Enterprise Board purchasing 99 per cent of the shares in the company. Over the next ten years £2,200 million of public money was invested in the company, roughly £120 for every family in the country.

Have we got our money's worth? We have certainly done better than if the company, now called Rover Group, had been closed. The unemployment pay and lost taxes would have cost the taxpayer well over £1,000 million *every year*, more than £600 per family by now. But what really matters is that BL has earned us a net balance on foreign trade of roughly £800 million per year.

As table 1 shows, in 1979 Ford contributed £60 million to our foreign earnings, while GM managed to lose us £100 million. In 1984, however, Ford and GM between them were losing us £1,100 million. Indeed, the entire deterioration in our balance of trade in cars over this period is due to the activities of Ford and GM, and not to increased imports from European and Japanese producers.

Table 1 UK balance of trade in motor cars (£m)

	1979	*1984*
BL (including Jaguar)	+800	+800
Ford	+60	−500
GM	−100	−600
Overall trade balance	−1,765	−2,665

Source: D. T. Jones, Science Policy Research Unit, unpublished data

The reason for the deficits incurred by Ford and GM is clear from table 2. Since 1973 both companies have taken to importing a significant proportion of components and vehicles from their plants in Europe. The behaviour of Ford and GM is obviously based on straightforward commercial interest, not malice. It's not that they dislike the British, or that they are engaged in a conspiracy against our trading performance.

Table 2   UK content of cars sold in the UK (%)

	1973	1984
BL (including Jaguar)	100	92
Ford	88	49
GM	89	22

Source: D. T. Jones, *The Import Threat to the UK Car Industry*, Science Policy Research Unit, 1985

Management in all companies will run their affairs in what they consider to be the best interests of the company, and if that obligation does not accord with the best interests of the British economy the results are a foregone conclusion. It is understandable, if regrettable, if the high interest rate, high exchange rate, deflationary policies of Mrs Thatcher's government persuade companies to produce outside the UK.

Governments, however, have a quite different obligation. Any British government that knows its duty must give primacy to the interests of the British economy. In the case of the car industry all the evidence points to Mrs Thatcher's government doing just the opposite. In terms of likely financial, technological, trade and employment cost to the economy and hence to the British taxpayer, their attempt to flog off BL in 1986 was not simply economically unwise, it was a downright betrayal of responsibility.

One of the mysteries of the controversy in early 1986 surrounding the proposed disposal of parts of BL was that while the government wanted to get rid of our company, bought and built up by the British taxpayers who are supposed to be so dear to Mrs Thatcher, so many hard-headed, commercially minded firms wanted to buy it. What they were after was clearly BL's market share and, most of all, BL's newly established techno-logical lead. The Prime Minister regularly cites the relatively small size of BL (in particular its 4 per cent of the European car market) as the key indicator of the terminal failure of the public sector company for which she has such obvious contempt. So there was a peculiarly vindictive logic in her plan to sell off the truck divisions and Land Rover, leaving a smaller, and, as far as the Prime Minister is concerned, yet more vulnerable BL to fend for itself, until such time as its performance had deteriorated sufficiently to defuse any fuss at getting rid of it.

It is crucial to the future of the motor industry in this country that it be recognized that in her view of BL (Rover Group), as in many other respects, the Prime Minister is hopelessly out of date. Modern, computer controlled, 'just-in-time' production lines, and the evident distaste of the car-buying public for uniformity, is bringing the era of the huge production run and the 'world car' to an end. Anyone who, like me, has visited the fac-tories will see that, despite its relatively small size, BL has invested heavily in modern robotics; and will see why, according to *Engineer* magazine, the Metro production line is the most effi-cient in Europe, and why other companies wanted to pick the fruit of 12 years of public investment, and the efforts of manage-ment, workers and research, development, and design teams.

Where size does matter in the car industry is in marketing, finance, and research and development. Successful marketing requires an extensive network of dealers and service centres, and, of course, a first-rate product to sell. For many years, as far as European truck sales were concerned, BL had neither. Now the truck division has an acknowledged technical lead and an excellent product, but instead of seeking joint marketing arrangements, and exploring the implications of information technology for marketing and servicing, the Tory government is still determined to sell off the truck division. We are now accustomed to such perversity and lack of patriotism. In other countries governments and business leaders, including those who are supposed to be Mrs Thatcher's fellow Conservatives, regard her generosity towards Britain's competitors with political disbelief and commercial delight.

The financial and R & D implications of scale in the motor industry, and indeed in virtually all manufacturing industries, are closely related. The motor industry is no longer about 'medium-tech' metal bashing. It is a high-tech industry, second only to aerospace in the large-scale application of new materials and new production methods. Innovation on this scale requires the commitment of enormous amounts of money for considerable periods of time, both for pure research (the outcome of which is uncertain) and for the application of science to production.

The British financial system has shown itself to be singularly incompetent in the provision of the requisite funds. If companies are too small, or insufficiently profitable in the short term, to generate the money themselves to design a new wing, or develop a ceramic engine, or devise a new robot production line, they have only the government to turn to. That, over decades, is how government has, by default of the financial system, acquired the often complementary jobs of financing innovation and restructuring inefficient companies.

The contrast drawn by Will Hutton[1] between BL and the Japanese company which produces Mazda cars is instructive in this respect. In 1974 BL's debts equalled its equity and it would have been forced into bankruptcy if the Labour government had not undertaken the rescue. In the same year Mazda's debts were *four times bigger* than its equity, its technology was out of date (it was lumbered with the gas-guzzling Wankel engine), and its car production was only two-thirds that of BL. It was not abandoned by its bankers. Instead they undertook the successful refinancing and restructuring of the company, which is now a success. Indeed, in the stimulating environment of the relatively fast-growing Japanese economy Mazda has done better than BL, which has had to cope with a slow-growing economy and a hostile government for most of its post-rescue life.

Despite these conditions, the rescue of BL has nevertheless gone quite well so far. BL has modernized its range of cars (partly in collaboration with Honda), has achieved excellent, proven production improvements, and has developed innovative solutions to the problem of expensive R & D. The collaboration with Honda spreads R & D costs and contributes to the development of an effective marketing organization. Meanwhile, the Computer Aided Design and Manufacture (CADCAM) research programme developed jointly with Warwick University has brought some of the most sophisticated applications of information technology to mass production and marketing anywhere in the world. Executives from German car companies are coming to BL to be trained. The Rover Group (BL) still has a long way to go, and the recovery and restructuring of the corporation has left a long dole queue in its wake. But the company has shown that, even in a very difficult political and economic environment, it can begin to succeed.

There are a number of lesssons to be learned from the experience of BL, and from the business strategies pursued by Ford and GM.

First, in evaluating the cost to the nation of maintaining production it is necessary to make an assessment that is more in accord with the true cost to the economy rather than narrow short-term accounting criteria. Of course, commercial companies should be profitable in the long run. But short-term profits and losses can be very misleading guides to the best interests of the company and the nation.

Secondly, the need for a long-term view is particularly important in an industry like vehicle manufacture whose technological base is changing so rapidly that it sweeps much conventional commercial wisdom aside.

Thirdly, new technology requires both large sums of long-term money, and a mechanism whereby companies which are being badly run or have fallen on hard times can be restructured financially, managerially and technologically. In Britain this restructuring has either been done by the market (which has a distinctly short-term, non-constructive view) or, in a rather *ad hoc* manner, by the government.

Fourthly, the greatest challenge facing the motor-car industry, indeed all British industry, is the development and application of new materials and techniques. The enormous cost of these processes requires that research proceeds on a more collaborative basis, with more encouragement for 'research clubs' in which firms and government collaborate in pure and applied research. It is vital for the future of Britain that new ideas spread rapidly, in a coherent and co-ordinated manner, both within and between industries.

Fifthly, the activities of companies which move their production abroad have both a direct impact on employment in Britain – the loss of jobs in their own and in their suppliers' factories – and an indirect impact, for the resulting deficit on the balance of trade forces the government to deflate the economy (or to grow less rapidly) leading to jobs being lost elsewhere. We thus have a very clear formula for evaluating the performance of such companies operating in Britain: if their operations are producing a trade balance equal to or better than the average balance in their industry, and that balance is growing and likely to grow for the foreseeable future, then the operations of the company are *a priori* in the interests of Britain. If, however, a company's operations are leading to a trade balance which is worse than the average for the industry and that balance is worsening, then, other things being equal, the operations of the company are *not* in the best interests of Britain. In the latter case it is the responsibility of government to take appropriate action to rectify the situation.

Whatever happened to the sunrise?

As the decimation of British industry proceeded apace in the early years of Mrs Thatcher's government the Tories took to arguing that this was a 'natural' process, a consequence of the exploitation of North Sea oil; and this fairy-tale was buttressed by further arguments to suggest that not only was the process 'natural', it was also desirable. Surplus labour was being 'shaken out' as firms desperately cut costs to survive, and the companies which were disappearing were those in the 'old' industries, such as 'metal-bashing', which didn't belong in modern, post-industrial Britain. They would be replaced by the knowledge-intensive, 'sunrise' industries, the industries of the future, particularly electronics and information technology.

Not even that was true. The impact of Tory economic policy has resulted in a severe weakening of Britain's efforts in these crucial new industries. The manufacturing depression has robbed the British high-technology industry of the buoyant home market which it desperately needs to provide an environment within which expensive and risky research and development may be pursued. The policy toward high-technology industries in particular has been fragmented, incoherent, and desperately underfunded. On top of all that, basic research in the universities has been severely cut back.

The result is that a surplus on trade in data processing and telecommunications equipment of £100 million in 1979 has been turned into a deficit of £1,250 million in 1985. In the electrical and electronic engineering sector the share of imports has risen from 31 per cent to 46 per cent. In office machinery and computers the share of imports has risen from 92 per cent to 110 per cent, that is, we import more than we buy for use in Britain because many of our exports are really just re-exports of foreign-made equipment. At the same time our shares of world markets in high-tech products, *and in the services associated with high-tech products, such as software development*, have fallen steadily.

The importance of high technology to Britain's industrial future cannot be overstated. The influence of information technology (IT) in particular is being felt across all industries and throughout public and private services. The division between 'sunrise' and 'sunset' industries is totally bogus. A significant example of the impact of information technology can be found in the clothing industries. Companies like Benetton have used computer-aided design and management techniques to transform the industry, restoring the competitive lead to advanced countries. Yet the trade performance of the high-technology industries is indicative of a general malaise. A 1984 report by the National Economic Development Council argued that 'on present trends the UK will not have an independent broad-based IT industry by the end of the decade'.

The British electronics and IT industry is dominated by six companies: GEC, Ferranti, Plessey, Racal, Thorn–EMI, and STC. Their activities are, in turn, dominated by defence contracts. In the case of Ferranti, 51 per cent of total sales are defence sales; in the case of Racal 39 per cent, Plessey 37 per cent, GEC 20 per cent, STC 11 per cent and Thorn–EMI 9 per cent. The emphasis on military contracts and on military research and development has not only limited the development of commercially viable products, but also has induced a reluctance to take commercial risks, especially where the long-term uncertainties of innovative research are involved.

GEC, Britain's largest electronics company with a turnover in 1984 of £6,000 million, and a research budget of over £600 million, has failed to capture markets in such key high-technology fields as semi-conductors and robotics, preferring short-term profitability in commercial markets rather than investing for a long-term return. Similarly, Dr Alan Shepherd, the managing director of Ferranti Electronics, has argued (*Financial Times*, 28 September 1985) that Ferranti could not be a world leader in semi-conductors because 'we cannot afford to go for growth at the expense of high profitability'. The company is constrained from taking an 'adventurous' approach by the need to maintain loyalty to its shareholders.

It would be totally unfair to indict all the British companies in this sector for lack of long-term innovative commitment. Thorn–EMI have made major efforts in civilian areas. Yet the impact of the defence market and, until recently, the equally secure telecommunications market, seem to have induced a general corporate lethargy. Steady growth and profits have not been accompanied by commercial aggression, particularly in export markets. Demand is not enough. Other stimulus to innovation is needed.

An important role in the British market is played by multi-national companies, the most important of which is IBM, which was responsible for over 30 per cent of the value of total shipments of computer products to the UK in 1985. IBM claims that its impact on Britain's trade balance is broadly neutral – its imports being roughly balanced by its exports – and places great store on the research and development work done in the UK.

The comparative failure of the British companies to assume technological leadership in commercial fields has forced the government to play a major role. Support for ICL (owned since 1984 by STC) and for Inmos (owned since 1984 by Thorn–EMI) ensured a national presence in mainframe computers and in semi-conductors. Unfortunately, the privatization of both companies is likely to see them, for financial reasons, sharing with foreign companies the technical expertise built up with public investment.

The Alvey programme, launched in 1983, was designed to link government funding (£200 million taken from other government-funded research) with private finance (£150 million) in collaborative 'pre-competitive' research, by companies and university departments, in crucial commercial areas in which British expertise was clearly lacking. This is an important programme, though it has displayed an alarming tendency to shift toward military research. Whether it is a commercial success will depend on the second stage of the project. At the moment the emphasis is on pure research.

The Alvey idea is sound, but the execution has been imperfect. The government's emphasis on the need for companies to provide matching funds has restricted the access of the small firms which are often the source of the brightest ideas. The emphasis on collaboration has tended to stunt strategic thinking, a weakness which may become more evident at the second stage. Nonetheless, the very idea that the government should initiate collaborative research is a step forward. What is required now is that it should be linked to a coherent industrial policy.

The NEDC report on information technology pointed out that the development of high-technology industry in Britain is hampered not only by insufficient investment in research and innovation, but also by a severe shortage of well-trained workers at all levels. There is also a distinct lack of suitable venture capital for small and medium-sized firms who have the bright ideas which will require long-term investment. Funding is important not only for new products, but for the turnaround of companies with bright ideas which have got into financial difficulties. Money and managerial expertise for the latter task is in notably short supply.

All the lessons from the generally gloomy 'sunrise' sector point to the need for a strategic approach to the high-technology industries – in finance, in training, in research and development, and, perhaps most important of all, in public purchasing, the need to pursue the objective of commercial viability must be kept to the fore. Government policy must go beyond 'oiling the wheels of industry' or 'filling in the gaps in the market'. Military purchasing must be less self-indulgent. Public sector purchasing must be geared to wider markets. And the vital position of British Telecom as the major customer for telecommunications equipment must be exploited in the strategic development of British industry. Similarly, the utilization of the new technologies in all sectors of industry must be both encouraged and *guided*, the growth of demand used as a springboard to commercial innovation.

HOW DID OTHER COUNTRIES MANAGE TO DO SO MUCH BETTER?

Britain's share of world manufactured exports slid steadily downwards from the mid-fifties onwards, with only the 1974–9

Why Manufacturing?

Labour government having any success in stopping the rot.
Even that government's industrial policies were severely
hampered by short-term financial problems and industrial
relations difficulties. While Britain's share was falling, France
and West Germany managed to maintain their shares of world
trade (West Germany at about 19 per cent, France at about
9 per cent), Italy increased its share by more than a third (from
5.5 per cent to about 7.8 per cent, so *overtaking* Britain as an
exporter of manufactured goods) and Japan tripled its share
(from about 6.5 per cent to 19 per cent). By holding or increasing their shares of the world market these countries parti-
cipated fully in the huge growth of world trade which took
place in the fifities and sixties, and the consequences of the
much slower growth of world trade in the seventies and
eighties have been less severe for them than for Britain, whose
share has been falling.

How did they manage to do so well? And what lessons can we
learn from their experiences as we fashion our recovery strategy
in the depressed eighties?

At first sight, the economic policies adopted by France, Japan
and West Germany since the Second World War look very
different from one another.

The French adopted a highly centralized system of planning,
using a variety of *direct* measures – providing finance, varying
tax incentives and penalties, using tariffs and other trade
barriers to protect domestic industry, nationalizing some key
firms and taking substantial state holdings in others – to guide
the development of French industry.

The Japanese have adopted a similar strategic approach to
their international trade, but foster far more vigorous competition in their domestic markets. The fact that all basic materials
and all fuels have to be imported into Japan, and that in the
fifties and sixties most technology was also imported by the
purchase of foreign patents, gave the Ministry of International
Trade and Industry, which controlled imports either directly or
via the provision of foreign exchange, the supreme ability to

86

manipulate the structure of the economy. There has also been a history of the closest co-operation between government and industry in research and development. And, of course, there has been a very close relationship between industrial companies and their banks. The bank is typically the nucleus of the *keiretsu* (the successors of the old *zaibatsu*), the flexible grouping of affiliated, complementary companies, falling under the wing of the general trading company which plays the leadership role in charting new directions for the group.

In West Germany, in marked contrast to France and Japan, the government has consistently declared its adherence to the free-market doctrine of the 'social-market economy' spelt out in the early fifties by Ludwig Erhardt. But appearances can be deceptive. A dominant economic notion in post-war Germany, an idea raised almost to the level of an economic philosophy, is the idea of consensus, the desire to build a common sense of direction in government, finance, industrial management and the trade unions. This idea is not just an informal hope. It achieves concrete form in the very close relationship among the three great German industrial banks, which by their extensive equity participation in German industrial companies and their propensity to invest in long-term industrial development have become a force for the sponsoring of research and technical innovation, and for intra-industry co-ordination and rationalization. The state has also played a far more active role than is commonly appreciated. In the crucial years of the early sixties, when today's pattern of world trade was being established, the West German government provided discriminatory subsidies to trade and industry that were four times greater than British subsidies. And at the level of the firm, the building of a consensus between companies' management and workers is greatly aided by the fact that workers have seats on every company's *Aufsichtsrat*, the supervisory board which plans the long-term strategy of the company.

Despite the ostensible differences in these approaches, there are a number of common themes running through the divergent institutions and policies of the successful countries, and those themes contain important lessons for Britain.

First, in all successful countries there has been a commitment to a long-term view of industrial development, and therefore, a commitment to managing the market, that is, to eliminating, as far as possible, the harmful, short-run vagaries of so-called free markets. This is evident both in government industrial policies and in the long-term view taken by financial institutions. The companies in the successful countries are mercifully free of the persistent pressure to achieve short-term financial results, earnings in each quarter declared to be higher than the quarter before, which the Stock Exchange imposes on British companies and on the managers of institutional investment funds.

A particularly impressive example of commitment to the long term has been seen in the record of the Mitterrand government in France. The initial expansionary drive of the Mitterrand administration was cut short by problems on the foreign exchanges. The new socialist government in France went running for expansion and got mugged. A more cautious approach was then adopted and, in classic style, Mrs Thatcher said that François Mitterrand and his ministers were converts to her cause. The slowdown after the dash brought some depression and the French electorate fell for the sub-Thatcherite promise of the French right-wing parties in the 1986 election. It was an undeserved defeat, for despite the short-run difficulties of 1981–3, the French government maintained its ambitious programme for industrial modernization, particularly in the new technologies, and the fruits of this are now coming through.

There are, of course, political as well as economic lessons to be learned here. When faced with short-run difficulties, British governments have been all too ready to cut investment while preserving consumption. When they are not whining about pay rates, Mrs Thatcher, Lord Young, Mr Lawson and Mr Tebbit positively glory in the levels of consumption now being achieved by some of those in work, while presiding over crippling cuts in industrial investment. They are quite happy to jeopardize the future of Britain in the pursuit of what they believe will yield short-term electoral gain and give them some excuse to claim that the imaginary 'recovery' is under way.

In stark contrast to this Tory profligacy, the Mitterrand government, when faced with short-run difficulties, had the courage to keep its industrial and R & D investments going, even though this meant cutting the rate of growth of consumption. The results were politically painful even though the steadfastness was essential to the medium and long-term economic interests of France and the French people. As my party knows only too well, elections are often about the short term rather than the long term. Frankly, I do not believe that experience at home and abroad can be allowed to deter us from pursuing the long-term recovery strategy that we know to be essential in the best interests of Britain.

Together with my colleagues, therefore, I consider that it is vital to demonstrate continuously the crucial interdependence between our two-year jobs priority programme, a four- to five-year Medium Term Employment Strategy, and a ten-year Economic Planning Perspective. Those relationships and the disciplines on government that go with them are both, I believe, essential to the future of standards of living and liberty in our country. They cannot be left to the luck of the market or the kindness of competitors. They have to be worked for, planned for, and paid for. And if all of that is done and the electorate still feels that there is a softer option, that is their privilege in a democracy. They can then face their own children and contemporaries in 15 or 20 years' time and explain why they preferred short-term sweetness to the longer-term strategies that in our country above all industrial countries are vital to industrial survival and social progress. While it would be foolish and untrue to claim that we should somehow be 'above politics', I do say that the plight of the British economy is such that we are just going to have to get on with the changes that are needed, even though they are unlikely to bring quick success or easy popularity.

The need for a long-term view brings with it the second

characteristic of policy in the successful countries: a strategic approach to industrial development. This is clearly evident in French planning and German consensus. But it was particularly well described in a speech given in 1970 by Vice Minister Ojimi, of the Japanese Ministry of Trade and Industry. When I was first given a copy of this speech by the director of a small Japanese-owned plastics factory in my constituency in 1972, I thought that it was the best short answer I had seen to the question 'What should we do?'

> After the war [said Ojimi], Japan's first exports consisted of such things as toys or other miscellaneous merchandise and low-quality textile products. Should Japan have entrusted its future, according to the theory of comparative advantage, to these industries characterized by intensive use of labour? That would perhaps be rational advice for a country with a small population of 5 or 10 million. But Japan has a large population. If the Japanese economy had adopted the simple doctrine of free trade and had chosen to specialise in this kind of industry, it would almost permanently have been unable to break away from the Asian pattern of stagnation and poverty, and would have remained the weakest link in the free world, thereby becoming a problem area in the Far East.
>
> The Ministry of International Trade and Industry decided to establish in Japan industries which require intensive employment of capital and technology, industries that in consideration of comparative cost should be the most inappropriate for Japan, industries such as steel, oil refining, petro-chemicals, automobiles, aircraft, industrial machinery of all sorts, and electronics, including electronic computers. From a short-run, static viewpoint, encouragement of such industries would seem to be in conflict with economic rationalism. But from a long-range viewpoint, these are precisely the industries where income elasticity of demand is high, technological progress is rapid, and labour productivity rises fast. It was clear that without these industries it would be difficult to employ a population of 100 million and raise their standards of living to that of Europe and America . . .[2]

What seemed to me to be really important in Mr Ojimi's remarks was not his list of industries, but the strategic view which underpinned his approach. It had such obvious common sense and was so clearly backed up by 15 or 20 years of systematic success, that it was bound to beckon anyone who shared my frustration with the lack of coherence in most British economic policy, and the self-righteous anarchism of Britain's financial institutions. I knew, of course, that Mr Ojimi was no socialist. But even if he wasn't, he seemed to me, to paraphrase General Booth, to be a devil with a damned good tune that we could and should transcribe to British conditions, arrange to British needs, and play with gusto.

The appeal of that strategic approach was not neatness or conformity or uniformity, the characteristics which some of socialism's less thoughtful friends and all of its enemies claim for socialism. The appeal was in the cogency of a *plan*, though Mr Ojimi might not use the word. It had a flexible and powerful institution like MITI, which understood that location of modern industries can, other than in exceptional cases where climate or geology still dictate, be largely determined by the 'intensive employment of capital and technology' (and the people that use both) and which matched together those long-term capital resources, an audacious but realistic world market awareness, technical skills, and a real attitude of enterprise in a comprehensive strategy. There were no excuses about 'bottlenecks' or institutional inhibitions, no alibis about 'not being in this business before', no fear of failing so strong as to stop them trying. The fact that it worked was obvious, otherwise I wouldn't be reading Ojimi's speech in a Japanese-owned, unionized, decently paying, securely employing, plastic extrusion plant in South Wales in 1972. Neither would Aiwa be making electronic hardware in another part of my constituency in 1986. Nor would Japanese industry be generating a balance-of-payments surplus so huge and self-sustaining that Prime Minister Nakasone feels obliged to appeal to his citizens to buy foreign goods.

I would not suggest that the Japanese example or Japanese

conventions or institutions could or should be installed in the British body economic. Neither would I suggest that we commission a search for industries with 'comparative costs' that are 'inappropriate' for Britain or show a bold defiance of 'economic rationalism'. On the contrary, I would insist that there is little purpose and less need to be so venturesome. It would make more sense to play to our strengths, to invest in them, to train and research for new strengths, and to have the sense and patience to persist with all of that in pursuit of returns in the medium and long term. All I would seek to copy and implant with full vigour is the consistent strategy operated with and for partisan national interest.

In all the successful countries the strategic approach to industrial policy has been reinforced, indeed made practicable, by a financial sector which was also willing to take a long-run view. The third lesson to be learned from others' experience, therefore, is about the virtues of close links between finance and industry. In Britain the relationship has always been somewhat distant. This is not merely a question of the provision of finance, though the *Crédit National* and the *Crédit d'Equipement des Petites et Moyennes Entreprises* in France, and the *Kreditanstalt für Wiederaufbau* in Germany, have greatly facilitated the flow of finance to the small and medium-sized companies in which many of the new technologies are developed. Of equal importance has been the role which financial institutions have played in the re-organization and reconstruction of badly managed enterprises, or even of whole sectors which have fallen on hard times. British financial institutions are generally incapable of fulfilling this task. The terminal task of the receiver is more in evidence here than the constructive strategic assistance provided by industrial banks abroad.

A fourth lesson which emerges from the experience of Germany and Japan concerns the need to foster good industrial relations, involving the labour force in the planning of change. Rapid economic development necessarily involves disruption: tasks are changed, old skills become redundant and new skills must be learnt. Change can be exciting and fulfilling, or it can be threatening and destructive. The participation of the workforce in the management of industrial development is a key ingredient of an efficient development strategy. Building a social and economic consensus does not mean establishing conformity or insisting on subordination. Rather, it involves constructing a framework of industrial relations in the widest sense – covering not only pay and conditions within the individual firm, but also growth and development strategies at firm, industry and national level – a constructive framework within which differences can be hammered out and agreements forged that create the social fabric of our growing industry, providing well-paid, interesting jobs. Some will – do – argue that those arrangements require the surrender of free trade unionism. Few German or Japanese trade union activists would concur.

A fifth characteristic of industrial policies in the successful countries has been the perceived need to provide assistance not only on the supply side – ensuring that funds and resources are available – but on the demand side too. The Germans refer to demand-side policies as 'supply support' policies. In France and Japan trade restrictions have been used to direct demand toward those industries which the government wished to see prosper. Even today, within the bounds of EEC prohibition of trade barriers, more than 60 per cent of French imports are subject to non-tariff restrictions of one form or another, compared with the 15 per cent of British imports subject to non-tariff restrictions. The industrial growth and development in the home market provides the springboard into international markets.

Finally, it is abundantly clear that the success of France, Germany and Japan, and the difficulties of Britain, are not unrelated to the very different rates of investment that have persistently prevailed in these countries. Japan has invested around 30 per cent of its gross domestic product every year for the past 30 years. France and Germany have invested annually around 22 per cent of their gross domestic products over the same period. In Britain the rate of investment has been around

18 per cent, and is now down to 16.5 per cent under Mrs Thatcher's government. The plain fact is this: that unless we can improve the scale of our investment effort, in machines, in ideas, and in people; unless we introduce effective strategic policies to ensure that the quality of that investment is the highest possible, we shall simply be overwhelmed in today's competitive trading environment.

WHERE DO WE GO FROM HERE?

As the old joke goes, I'd rather not start from here. The rundown of our industrial economy has proceeded to such a destructive extent that the fears of the House of Lords Select Committee of 'a contraction of manufacturing to a point where the successful continuation of much of manufacturing activity is put at risk' are not so far from being realized. But recovery *is* possible. If we put manufacturing first; if we re-orient our economic perspectives away from narrow short-run financial calculation; if we fit monetary policy, and taxation policies, and trade policies to the needs of manufacturing, instead of forcing manufacturing into a straitjacket of totally inappropriate fiscal and monetary policies, then we can recover. We can create jobs – real, sustainable, long-term jobs. And we can begin to build a better society.

The key is industrial policy, strategic planning, and the construction of a framework of social and industrial co-operation within which *all* British people can join in the task of rebuilding our country.

NOTES

1   Will Hutton, *The Listener*, 13 February 1986.
2   John Eatwell, *Whatever Happened to Britain?* (Duckworth/BBC, 1982), pp. 89–90.

5
Planning Our Recovery

If policies continue on the present course the British economy will, in the next decade or less, move into a deepening decline in which standards of living fall steeply, even for many who now feel themselves to be safe, prospects for our children become limited and insecure, and the very stability of our society and our democracy is eroded. We don't, as Aneurin Bevan would say, have to look into the crystal ball; we can read the book or, more exactly, recall the experience of recent years.

We have already had a bitter taste of what could come. In the midst of the biggest revenue bonanza which any British government has ever enjoyed, the Tories have depressed, divided and embittered Britain. Young people have been impoverished and alienated. The old have been deprived and neglected. Every effort has been made to promote that extremity of selfishness which is the distinguishing feature of today's Toryism.

Those efforts have failed. Amongst the strongest reasons for the widespread antagonism to the policies and attitudes collectively called 'Thatcherism' has been the instinctive hostility which British people of all political affiliations have felt for the callousness of the creed favoured by the Prime Minister and those who do her bidding. The reaction has not been because of the 'wetness' which Mrs Thatcher scorns. It is evidence of the residual strength of the British people, and that sense of justice, of 'fair play', is not a maudlin sentimentality but a fundamental attribute. However, while that strength is resilient, it is not a superhuman benevolence. It is not incapable of being eroded by the continual pressures of economic decline. It would indeed be foolish and romantic of anyone to suppose that even in Britain prolonged economic insecurity cannot produce resentment among sufferers, and anxiety among those who believe themselves to be threatened by it. Fear, prejudice and aggression are the products of that combination. And then, if the experience of impoverishment and insecurity is wide enough, neither the noble generosity of the poor, nor the conscience-stricken philanthropy of the rich, is enough to limit those feelings to an 'anti-social' fringe.

If nothing is done to begin a significant change of course in our economic affairs, then the tightening grip of balance-of-payments deficits – no longer cushioned by oil revenues and worsened by deficits in trade in manufactures – will further squeeze the life out of our economy and depress the living standards of our people. On present policies it is now no exaggeration to anticipate unemployment rising to more than five million, and the pressures of financial and environmental poverty intensifying and multiplying until, partly as a result of idleness and ill-being arising from these circumstances, crime and social violence rise even above the record levels presided over by Mrs Thatcher.

Mrs Thatcher, in synthetic anger, condemns those who see a relationship between deprivation and delinquency as offering an 'insult to the unemployed'. It isn't, and she and they know it. The raw fact is that unemployment and poverty give extra time and temptation for crime and the vicarious thrills of vandalism and violence. They are not excuses – there aren't any. They are merely obvious reasons for some of the increase in such offences and they are reasons that are capable of being reduced by the operation of policies which take away much of the time and the temptation. There is no neat list of reasons for the increase in violence and hooliganism, and no perfect set of cures. It is clear, however, that particular crimes have increased and are increasing in parallel with unemployment, insecure employment and other factors which foster the view that large numbers of people are neither employed, valued or cared about. That sour view may be wrong but it is now deeply rooted. And if practical efforts with tangible results are not made to increase employment and opportunity and prove the error of that view, it and the criminality which breeds it will spread.

The reality of the possibility, made all the more menacing by the measured words used by, among others, the House of Lords Select Committee on Overseas Trade, demands a fundamental change of direction.

Obviously part of that change must be manifested in social policies. Acts of rescue are necessary for some whose plight is so pitiful and poverty so extreme that they form an underclass. Acts of stimulus and support are necessary for those whose potential will never be discovered, let alone fulfilled, if they are neglected much longer. But we face the fact that such policies, while vital, cannot be long sustained if other changes are not made to promote the creation of wealth to fund the improvement of support. That is just one of the basic reasons for insisting that industrial policy commands priority in the next Labour government. Improved *distribution* of wealth, however necessary and justifiable, cannot long exceed improved *production* of wealth.

THE OBJECTIVES OF INDUSTRIAL POLICY

The Tory government of Margaret Thatcher bears a major part of the responsibility for the difficulties which are engulfing Britain; but the sources of weakness obviously existed years before Thatcherism turned crumble into collapse.

Since the fifties governments should have been acting persistently to change the structure of our economy and the rules of the game by which economic policy is conducted. They plainly have not, although not for want of periodic exhortation. Advances made in improving the competitiveness of British industry – largely as a result of Labour government efforts to attend to underinvestment and price disadvantages – were neither sufficient to secure freedom from Britain's continual balance-of-payments constraints, nor given institutional or industrial roots deep enough to withstand a subsequent dose of Tory incompetence and profligacy. It wasn't just that the advances were lost on the electoral roundabouts. It was that each Tory government – and the Thatcher government more ruinously than any – zealously dismantled what elements of planning and continuity had been established, whether they were in infant institutional shape or in the more general form of investment incentives, training and technology funds or trade support. Given the present condition of the economy, and its acknowledged prospects if policies continue unchanged up to the end of Mrs Thatcher's seventh year, the historic habit must be broken. That is why the Labour Party will implement the three-stage integrated recovery programme of a two-year emergency jobs initiative, a five-year Medium Term Employment Strategy and a ten-year Economic Planning Perspective. We need very deliberately to sponsor recovery and also to ensure that it has deep roots, both for the purpose of achieving perceptible economic advance in the medium term and to provide a basis for continual change and improvement in our national and international performance.

That approach is not produced by caution or timidity. It comes from a realistic calculation of the needs and the options. If the initial jobs programme were to fail to stimulate demand and employment to the degree necessary then the growth rate of the economy would be too slow to carry us through to sustainable expansion in the medium and longer term. If we splurge out on a Heath–Barber style 'dash for growth' then we will reap the whirlwind of balance-of-payments problems, inflation and a domestic financial crisis. That would clearly weaken our effort to secure a long-term recovery for manufacturing industry. Industrial policy measures, low interest rate financing, strategic government and industry investment plans, and technology strategies would all be knocked back by the blows to confidence and consensus. If our longer-term industrial strategy were to 'underachieve', if we were to fail to make a clear start in modernizing our industrial capacity, our education and training, our R & D and our industrial relations, and if we were to fail to begin to recover the international competitiveness that the Tories have lost, then the short-term employment gains of the first two years will be steadily eroded.

The conundrums and colliding pressures are obvious – but they must be faced, not dodged. Since it is clear that in all three stages of the strategy a tight resource constraint will exist because of the weak balance-of-payments position which we will inherit, all industrial policy must be formulated, implemented and monitored specifically to attain a sustainable trend of improvement in the balance of trade and payments in manufacturing industry. That is the way to pursue our object of high and rising levels of employment in the economy as a whole, both in the industries where trade and sales are expanding and more generally, because of the wider effects of increased growth and income.

The pressures of the balance of payments have previously given rise to policies of deflation. We must now respond to them with policies of investment and expansion, implemented at a pace and on a system of priorities that enables the country to produce its way to surplus and the employment of labour and capital that goes with it instead of contracting into further trouble as we pursue the self-defeating course of shrinking our way to a solvency that never comes.

The criteria for evaluating the progress of such policies will not simply be short-term fluctuations in the balance-of-payments statistics. The task of new building and rebuilding in Britain's industries is now so great and so essential that it will have to be persisted with and not periodically halted by short-term pressures. It is not a matter of boom or bust. It is a matter of steadily and surely sustaining expansion –or going broke. The advances made in trade, and in investment, production and employment – these must be the criteria for the evaluation and selection of industrial programmes by the economic ministries, and these will be the guide to the actions of all other government departments which impinge on manufacturing industry.

These criteria will, of course, be applied within a framework of economic expansion. I have already noted that any fool can secure a positive balance of trade and payments by depressing the home economy far enough. Our objective is a steadily improving trade performance at any given level of output, which provides the wherewithal for expanding the level of output.

Plainly, the criteria beg some questions. It is quite conceivable, for instance, that an investment which would lead to a long-run improvement in the trade position would nevertheless precipitate a short-run deterioration as necessary inputs are imported. When applied to the activities of a single firm, such action may give a misleading impression of that firm's role in the drive to improve competitiveness. For example, an expansion of Britain's clothing industry leading to an improvement of that industry's international balance may well lead to a deterioration in the international trade balance of English Sewing Limited, the company which produces most of Britain's cotton thread and which must necessarily import most of its raw materials. That would obviously not discredit the company or the strategy. Getting the means to feed expansion is completely different from importing finished and part-finished goods because we've stopped making them.

I believe that these qualifications serve not to weaken but to strengthen the fundamental policy criteria. The fact that short-run and long-run effects have to be taken into account, and that the interrelationships between different firms and sectors require a broad, integrated view of the production process, emphasizes the power and width of the 'trade balance' criteria. Application of the criteria raises the questions which must be asked and answered if the overall trade balance in manufacturing is to be improved.

What if the criteria are applied to non-manufacturing industries or firms? Clearly we want to improve Britain's trade balance in tourism. An increase in the number of foreign tourists in Britain, although it would lead to an expanded demand for manufactures (everything from furnishings to catering equipment, and from double-decker buses to buildings) obviously need not lead to any deterioration in the manufactures balance by 'pushing out' manufacturing.

The issue is not so clear cut, however, in the case of those service sectors whose activities impinge very directly on the productive health of manufacturing. In the awful days of the early eighties when business failures and closures were occurring at an alarming rate, the Bank of England stepped in on many occasions to save companies which the commercial banks would have condemned to failure. The lending rules of the commercial banks were then clearly harmful to the long-term prospects of British manufacturing, and thus to the long-term prospects of the British economy, even though they may have seemed to be in the best, most prudent, interests of the banks themselves. If the latter is indeed the case, then the financial rules of the commercial banks are inappropriate to the long-term interest of Britain and must be changed.

Another important instance arises when the investment activities which are perceived to be in the best interests of a financial institution are plainly not in the best interests of manufacturing industry. Such an example would arise when a financial institution decided to invest substantially abroad since it believed that investment strategy to be most profitable in the short term. If that foreign investment imposed a strain on the balance of payments which led to deflationary pressure at home and a reduced rate of growth of domestic manufacturing, then, by our criteria, the investment is harmful. When there is a clear divergence of private and public benefit, of narrow corporate interest and of broad national interest, it is obvious that the needs of our country for investment must come first, not as a matter of jealousy or vindictiveness, but as a matter of

101

productive necessity. Mrs Thatcher seems to have the delusion – at least she tries to foster the illusion – that the substantial increase in the export of capital since 1979 is beneficial because of the income which it provides for 'us' – a sort of nest egg to fund the days after we retire from oil production. Apart from the fact that what returns do come back from this source are unlikely to end up as NHS hospitals or old age pensions, the idea that a country like ours can to any significant extent live off lending is ridiculous, especially when in the very act of providing resources for others we are emaciating our own industrial economy.

Industrial policy and the needs of industrial development cannot depend upon the fragile possibility that individuals and institutions suddenly take it into their heads to make investment resources available in the right quantity, at the right price and for the necessary time because they've had a fit of patriotism. Neither can the needs for domestic investment now be met out of the earnings from foreign investment. Industrial development requires that capital resources in Britain are used in Britain, and while there will obviously continue to be capital investment abroad, we have to reduce the flow significantly. Labour's capital repatriation scheme (see pp. 168–9) is designed to do exactly that.

THE NEED FOR PLANNING

No rational company would pursue even the most limited goals without careful planning and the pursuit of major reform must most certainly be carefully planned. Planning is necessary because a modern industrial economy must be organized within a long-run perspective. If programmes of investment in industrial capacity, research and training are not conducted and co-ordinated in the light of long-run objectives, then any hope of catching up with, let alone surpassing, our major competitors will vanish.

Planning must be strategic. This implies in turn that government action will be discriminatory. It's no good defining clear objectives, and then setting out to achieve them while pretending that all firms in all industries and all places are entitled to the same government support, the same tax incentives, the same subsidized loans. Our resources are limited and must therefore be targeted.

Planning must involve the people in industry who have the information and the skills to turn long-term planning strategies into productive reality. It must be a process which invites participation and builds a consensus aimed at the attainment of national objectives. It therefore requires the co-ordination of people and activity and enterprises, whose purposes are in accord with the objectives of the society as a whole, in order to assist them in achieving their own goals more effectively. Any satisfactory planning process must therefore be decentralized, the necessary coherence being achieved by clearly specified and agreed objectives and a well-organized flow of information throughout the economy.

Planning must be practical – it must mean pursuing those goals which can be attained, because the material means are available, because the people involved are ready and willing to do the job, and because the job needs to be done.

These ingredients cannot be satisfactorily provided by the market. The pressures of the market are essentially short-run. Managers of investment funds who attempted to make long-run strategic use of the investments under their control, and forego the opportunity to make short-run speculative gains which show up immediately in the quarterly statement, would (conventionally at least) be put out of their jobs. And the market does not build a consensus; it creates divisions.

Yet markets are, and will be, an enduring aspect of any modern, well-run industrial economy, and certainly the world economy will continue to be a marketplace. An efficient planning system uses the strengths of the market – the stimulus of competition, the response to consumer needs, the incentive to invention and effective commercial innovation – to attain national goals. Markets, as I said earlier, make far better servants than masters.

103

I have always found the traditional debates concerning markets versus planning to be irrelevant. The British economy will not cease to be a market economy just because it is planned strategically and focused on long-run national goals. The British economy will remain a market economy, both because the use of markets is in many cases an efficient way of achieving our goals, and because the abolition of markets for so many goods and services is a sectarian fantasy. Similarly I consider the blanket hostility which is fashionable in some circles to any form of planning to be a supersitition. The assertion that 'planning has never worked in Britain' is puerile, historically ignorant, and presupposes that the absence of planning *has* worked in Britain. Failure to plan and failure to plan properly has put us into the present mess, and the longer we go on like that the worse the mess is going to be.

It is a characteristic of uncontrolled markets that they establish vicious or virtuous circles of failure or success. In the virtuous version, success breeds success – although it can generally be seen that the jolly process was begun with some stringent and judicious planning. The British economy is caught in a vicious circle with low growth of demand for British goods leading to low profitability and investment, and so on. Breaking out of this vicious circle will require a well-organized *planned* effort, since it was always obvious (and is now painfully so) that the nineteenth-century liberal nostrum of leaving the markets to themselves which has been exhumed and operated by Mrs Thatcher's government is a pathetically inadequate basis for recovery.

THE FUNCTIONS OF PLANNING

The main contributions that we want from our planning system is an increase in the volume of investment and an improvement in its efficiency, where efficiency is defined as a trend improvement in the trade balance brought about by capturing markets at home and abroad. Any satisfactory planning system must fulfil four principal functions.

First, planning requires a central information function. In Britain we must identify, as other countries have done, the opportunities and the threats which face the various industrial sectors of our economy in the short term and in the long term. Then we need to select priority industries, even priority firms, in the light of potential competitive advantage, especially in high-quality production, which links in with existing strengths in research and training and which has the potential for long-term expansion. We must identify the capital requirements, the research and development needs, the skill shortages, and the marketing and design failings which inhibit expansion in our target industries. From this exercise we can derive a clear indication of the disaggregated components of the overall investment programme so that we have a chart and not just a destination.

The second planning function should be consultation to discover the investment, research and training plans of public companies and of large-scale private companies. We need to establish how their plans relate to growth and employment prospects, how far their corporate objectives and the wider national objectives are at one.

This leads on to the third planning function which is the negotiation and compilation of measures needed to gain the growth response from the private and public sector, the evaluation of specific public and private sector projects which the government is asked to support, and the auditing of earlier programmes to assess their effectiveness.

Fourth, the planning system must provide a framework for the implementation of suitable measures, whether this involves the provision of resources in grant, loan or allowance form, or advice and information, or whether it requires a more direct form of intervention by funding, partial or full ownership, the discriminatory use of the buying power of the public sector or international promotional activity.

These four functions must be performed as they have been

performed in *all* of the successful industrial economies. The institutional arrangements which have done the job differ considerably in precise form from one country to another because they have developed in economies with different industrial and cultural histories and conditions. The planning regimes, however, all perform the same functions, and it is that which we must emulate.

In Britain we are faced with the problem of finding institutions which can do the job, and which fit as well as possible into our way of doing things. The difficulty of doing this is compounded by the fact that we already have a fully-fledged set of economic institutions in place. It's not as if we were trying to transform a pre-industrial economy into an industrial economy (the environment in which the great German industrial banking system was formed) or trying to reconstruct an economy anew after the war (when much of the modern Japanese economic structure originated). Instead we have to change an existing, working system because it is working very badly. That is tougher. It is always more difficult to change an established convention than to surmount a new problem.

PLANNING AND PARTICIPATION

The central role in British strategic planning must be performed by a Department of Trade and Industry – but it must be a rather different DTI from the edifice we have at present.

The Tories have systematically weakened the DTI. It has been a revolving ministerial chair – Keith Joseph, Norman Tebbit, Cecil Parkinson, Leon Brittan and Paul Channon have all taken a turn in the past seven years, and at the same time the Thatcher government has cut back overall spending on industrial policy through the DTI from £3.2 billion in 1981–2 to £1.5 billion in 1984–5. Cutting spending on industrial programmes in half is hardly the act of a government which cares about British industry. The decline of manufacturing industry in Britain has not been something forced on the Tories by external circumstances, or even something they have passively accepted, it has been a decline in which they have actively connived.

But merely strengthening the DTI and its associated ministries in Wales, Scotland and Northern Ireland would not sufficiently alter the direction of industrial policy. The Department is at the present devoted to the *support* of industry, more than the *creation* of industry. Its entire posture has been far too passive, when what is needed is an active, entrepreneurial ministry, a ministry of movers, of new ideas, of new initiatives. It is not a question of believing that all, or even most, can be done by government acting through a ministry which is a mixture of think tank and piggy bank. It is again a matter of learning from the success of others who have forceful governmental agencies and use them to great economic advantage.

Future Neddies

While such a dynamic ministry can perform some of the information function required in planning, not least by adding a lot of information itself, it is not the best means of performing the consultation functions which are at the core of the planning process. Here there is a vital role for the National Economic Development Office (NEDO) and for the Little Neddies and the Sector Working Parties, not as a replay in committee making but as an essential framework for cohesion and co-ordination of information and activity.

NEDO is now a much reduced version of its former self, and but a shadow of what it was planned to be when it was established in 1962. Then it was hoped that NEDO would become a distinctly British version of the French *Commissariat Général du Plan*, a tripartite agency, bringing together management, trades unions and government to galvanize and guide Britain's industrial recovery. The organization has failed to live up to expectations partly because of the conventions of the environment in

107

which it has had to operate and partly because it has never been given the tools to do the job. Instead of being an organization that could plan, negotiate action, take initiatives and have real influence of the use of resources, it became just a consultative body – a talkshop, when what we need is a workshop. NEDO is valuable because it brings government, unions and management together, and pursues some important economic research (particularly at the level of individual industries). But it does not go beyond this limited brief, and any attempt at taking an independent pro-industry line has been impeded by the Treasury, which has had far too much influence on its activities.

But NEDO has survived. Even in the anti-industrial climate of the Thatcher years, battered and truncated, it has endured and, moreover, has produced some reports of major importance, such as that on the condition and potential of policies towards the high-tech industries which I have already mentioned. It has survived because both sides of industry have realized how important a forum like NEDO can be and because of the quality of its written output.

Its 24-year record has earned NEDO a reputation for being practical and perceptive, even though it has not been allowed to be operational in the way that it could and should usefully have been. That reputation should stand the Office in good stead in the new role that is now necessary. To do the job now required of it NEDO will have to change. At present its activities do not even cover the whole economy. Only about 32 per cent of GDP and 36 per cent of employment (comprising agriculture, construction, 60 per cent of manufacturing and 16 per cent of services) are covered. What is needed is a comprehensive extension of NEDO's activities to cover all manufacturing and all the major participants in industrial decision making, not only firms and trades unions and the central government, but also regional bodies and financial institutions. All these must also be involved in the Little Neddies and the Sector Working Parties which will be developed into sectoral planning bodies that can feed industrial ideas and information into the central forum. The Sector

Working Parties themselves will receive their information from joint trades union and management planning bodies established within the companies making up each sector.

NEDO will develop by this means into a decentralized, participatory planning structure, within which the people who really know what is going on in industry, the workers and management in the individual firms and sectors, can develop and apply a strategic plan for their firm and their industry. They won't be blankly told what to do. They can participate in planning what is to be done.

If such a participation is to result in efficient decisions being made, whether within the firm or the industry, there must be greater access to information. Of course, firms and industries differ in their organization. Some industries are dominated by large firms, others have many small firms. And some contain just one or two trades unions, whereas others have many unions. It would therefore be unreasonable to attempt to impose any rigid formula for consultation. Procedures can either evolve as a natural extension of collective bargaining, or a different constitutional framework can be adopted. The crucial thing is that they are there and working.

This decentralized, adaptable planning structure is basic to the success of strategic planning in the economy as a whole. But national decisions are obviously also vital to what is done at the industry level. The overall rate of growth of the economy, strategic decisions concerning priority industries, trade policies, interest rate policies – all affect the individual firm and each industry sector and must form the agenda of the National Economic Assessment. Through that means, and using the ideas and decisions of firms and industries, the economic possibilities and options facing the country will be reviewed, the overall distribution of national resources as between consumption, investment and government expenditure will be considered, and the implications for the overall industrial strategy assessed.

The transformed NEDO will be the key strategic agency in the formation of industrial policy. Its effectiveness will depend not only on its technical competence as an organization, but also on the commitment of all involved. That is why the Labour Party believes that the extension of industrial democracy can be a significant agency for greater efficiency.

MAKING THINGS HAPPEN

The main implementing agency which will have the task of carrying out the strategy compiled with NEDO will be the DTI. The package of measures available to the DTI must be rationalized to bear more directly on the primary objective of *industrial* policy – the steady improvement of trade performance in all sectors of industry. This policy objective will be applied in the context of established DTI measures such as investment support (where investment grants will be a major instrument) and competition policy (where the City's game of mergers musical chairs will be replaced by a coherent industrial strategy within which monopoly and mergers policy must be directed toward long-run trade performance).

But to promote the impetus needed properly some new approaches are required, approaches to uproot the complacency and hidebound convention of much of finance and industry in this country. The British Industrial Investment Bank and British Enterprise will pursue this task at national level. At the local level the regional development authorities will combine intimate knowledge of local strengths, weaknesses, needs and potential with access to the national investment and enterprise bodies to operate an active expansion programme that gets value for money and for the local economy.

The British Investment Bank

Britain has one of the most sophisticated financial systems in the world. It is highly skilled in financing trade, dealing in British and foreign government securities, dealing in the second-hand stocks and shares of British and foreign companies, and generally managing money and monetary instruments at home and abroad. It is far less skilled in or disposed to investing in production or in research or design. Few British financial institutions have the expertise typically found in German industrial banks to appraise the long-term significance of engineering or scientific projects. Nor have British financial institutions developed the German and Japanese practice of taking significant ownership stakes in industrial companies, and then participating actively in the organization of industrial management – not, at least, until the receiver is called in. They should be midwives; instead, they are undertakers.

The result of all this is that British financial institutions tend to have an arms length relationship with British industrial companies. Only about 15 per cent of long-term investment in Britain is financed by raising new money through the City of London. Most investment finance comes from ploughed-back profits and depreciation funds. This contrasts with the situation in France and Germany where up to half of long-term investment is financed by financial institutions, primarily the banks, and Japan, where the proportion of bank finance is even higher.

The debate over whether the characteristics of the relationship between British financial system have contributed to Britain's poor industrial performance is more than academic. We have a particular financial system which in its own terms is successful. And we have an unsuccessful industrial sector. Given the role which finance has in a capitalist economy of mobilizing resources – and must have in any economy in fuelling production – there must be some causal relationship between the relative success of one and the definite failure of the other. What is clear is that the British financial sector does not play the monitoring and restructuring role that the industrial banks do in other countries. Neither the merger mechanism nor bankruptcy procedures perform that task effectively. That is why in Britain it is so often left to the government to pick up the pieces. In these circumstances the contempt expressed for 'the City' by a wide

spectrum of opinion ranging from working managers and pres-
surized entrepreneurs to me and my fellow socialists is entirely
justified. Contempt, however, is no more useful than name-
calling. Change is what is needed.

And the need for that change is not mitigated by the finding of
the Wilson Committee that there was no general lack of finance
for British industry. When the pace of innovation and development in British industry is notoriously slow and limited the demands are proportionately small. The provision of funds is made
adequate mainly by the deficiency of demand. And apart from
that, there is also the fact that the experience of medium-sized
and small businesses – especially at the innovatory stages –
shows that the attitudes and practices of the conventional capital sources are a real inhibition to starting and a great burden on
continuing.

The role of the British Investment Bank will be to deal with
some of the financial aspects of this situation. Both the *Crédit
National* and the *Kreditanstalt für Wiederaufbau* invested more
than £1 billion in 1985 in the development of French and
German industry respectively. They invested in long-term projects, typically on rather favourable terms. The BIB will perform
the same role, seeking out and stimulating commercially viable
projects.

British industry will begin the task of innovative recovery in
circumstances that are obviously unpropitious. Financial
resources must be mobilized for companies and sectors trying to
recover from past records of poor profitability and productivity
and for long-term projects offering a return in the future rather
than a quick turnaround. There is thus a need for a venture capital
institution which will provide finance on favourable terms to
small and medium-sized businesses. It's not only a question of the
sums involved but their direction, too; the capital has to go to the
right firms in the right sectors to fit in with overall strategy.

The Bank will not only offer money. It should be able to offer
a comprehensive package of technical, managerial, marketing
and financial assistance, drawing on the resources of private

industry and the DTI. The aim is to construct an organization similar in scale and effect to the comparable French, German and Japanese institutions (the Japan Development Bank) which will act as the financial arm of an aggressive industrial strategy, offering cheap money and high commercial expertise.

British Enterprise

The British Investment Bank, as a venture capital institution, will not be able to play the role which the European industrial banks do in systematically reorganizing industry. It will be neither big enough nor sufficiently integrated (if integrated at all) with the large companies which dominate British manufacturing industry. The restructuring job will fall primarily to British Enterprise.

British Enterprise will be a state holding company which will complement the loan finance of the Investment Bank by taking equity stakes in companies pursuing the objectives of the industrial policy. The relationship between British Enterprise and the private sector will clearly be flexible, assuming any of a wide variety of forms depending on what is appropriate to the varying situations. In joint ventures British Enterprise will be able to take majority or minority stakes in existing or newly created companies. It could establish new companies, or simply arrange for managerial or technical expertise to be available to old ones. British Enterprise will take the lead for the government in operations to restructure industry and to rationalize production for the purpose of improving the quantity and quality of output.

As with all the industrial institutions, the activities of British Enterprise will be geared toward improving trade performance in manufacturing industry. Its major role will be to promote change in that direction.

Neither in this case or in any other do I or my colleagues work on the assumption that the creation of new institutions with great objectives is a replacement for the *action* necessary to innovate, to renew, to invest and produce. What is clear from experience at home and abroad, however, is that we must, like our major competitors, have such bodies to assemble experience and expertise, to focus on objectives, to assist in funding production, to participate in planning economic development and to promote the cohesion of economic activity. Without them there will be no structure for recovery other than that casually granted by the existing inadequate institutions with their short-term whims, their divorce from the real economy, their capricious lack of concern for the current or future interests of Britain and – irony of inevitable ironies – their defeat of the 'enterprise' at whose shrine they worship with such pious insincerity.

OPERATING ON THE DEMAND SIDE

The traditional approach adopted to industrial policy by the DTI has been to provide resources, to act on the supply side. Clearly, allocating resources efficiently is very important, and in this task the DTI, the British Industrial Investment Bank and British Enterprise have vital jobs to do.

But if there is no prospect of a sustained demand for a product then no amount of readily available resources will persuade a manager to invest. Firms produce in order to sell. If they don't expect to sell, they don't produce. Moreover, given the fact that modern industry must plan on the basis of a fairly long time-scale, novel and risky investment in new products and processes requires some confidence in the long-run maintenance of demand. The image of the debt-defying, risk-taking entrepreneur dashing from brilliant idea through temporary travail to millionaire success is, meanwhile, best left to the romantics and propagandists. The reality is nearer to people with good ideas and hard work double-mortgaging their homes to fund production that is expanded cautiously and sales that take a lot of slog.

A stable rate of growth of the economy as a whole – not

stagnation or sprints for growth – will make an important contribution to the prosecution of a successful industrial policy. But a discriminatory industrial strategy will be all the more effective if there can be demand side discrimination as well as supply side discrimination.

The way in which the Japanese have protected their home market by means of tariffs, quotas, exchange controls and a variety of less formal trade barriers is well known. Many of these barriers have now been dismantled since, given Japan's dominance in so many industries, they are no longer necessary. But in that crucial period when Japan was catching up with other industrial countries, the ability of the Ministry of International Trade and Industry to manipulate demand by controlling imports was a key part of the industrialization strategy. In the fifties the French used discriminatory import restrictions in much the same way as did the Japanese, while the Germans used export subsidies to boost demand for their industries.

Britain faces the problem that these powerful ways of manipulating demand and intervening in trade are now less practicable because of the changes in the world economic environment that have taken place since the fifties when Germany, France and Japan operated such policies. Although the United States uses trade controls while arguing vigorously against them (just as they practise super-Keynesianism at home whilst imposing super-monetarism abroad), the major industrial countries would react strongly against a British effort to replicate the tough trade protection and promotion policies which gave the Japanese, French and Germans a sound foundation for advance. The trade treaty which links all the major industrial countries, the General Agreement on Tariffs and Trade (GATT), is dedicated to the removal of trade barriers and only permits barriers to be erected in cases of 'fundamental disequilibrium'. The prohibition of trade restrictions is even more strict in the Treaty of Rome, which regulates trade policy within the EEC. And the EEC emphasis on free trade is being enhanced by Community moves toward 'completing the internal market', moves which are designed

115

not only to eliminate any trade barriers which still exist, but also, by removing all border controls, to sweep away the possibility of ever raising any trade barriers in the future.

The hostility to the use of controls on trade as part of an industrial strategy which is now professed by those very countries which used such controls to launch their own industrial success stories will not, however, deter us from using trade controls where they are necessary to ensure the success of our recovery strategy. In the motor industry, for example, there must be an expanding demand for British-made cars and British-made components. In electronics there must be that prospect of long-term demand which is the only basis for the needed investment in research and development.

Hostility to such selective measures from other countries is understandable but irrational. It is far better for them for Britain to be a modern, vigorous trading partner, than for the British recovery to fail due to lack of demand and the economy to decline into stagnation, thereby reducing their markets in Britain below the levels they could have attained.

There are a number of other measures the government can and must take to maintain the structure of demand (provide 'supply support') which do not infringe treaty obligations or bring with them the reaction which would stall expansion. Chief among these is the use of public purchasing. The government buys roughly one-fifth of all industrial output, and by using its enormous buying power in a discriminatory manner can greatly reinforce the modernization strategy. This is particularly important in the high-technology industries, where long-term public contracts provide a secure environment for investment in capacity, research and development and training. The United States government has been particularly skilful in the deployment of government purchasing power to aid new industries, primarily through the Defense Department.

The British government must be prepared to use its purchasing power in a similarly direct manner. Indeed, the DTI should take the initiative in consulting government departments on their spending plans to ensure the maximum benefit to the industrial strategy. Nationalized industries and other firms in which the government has an interest should also be encouraged to integrate their spending plans with the strategic objectives of the industrial policy. 'Batting for Britain' is a team game, not an excuse for excursions abroad by a Prime Minister who, through a variety of means, some deliberate, others merely daft, has opened Britain to the biggest ever incursion of finished foreign produce.

There are a variety of other measures which can be used to influence the structure of demand, particularly measures of the informal, non-tariff variety. British governments have not utilized all the options open to them in the past. This stand-off attitude is out of date. Roy Hattersley has suggested that we need to take a 'Marks and Spencer approach' to the management of demand. We must not simply 'Buy British', we must use the power of the purse to raise standards of quality and of production so that everyone else wants to buy British.

Retailing is a very efficient industry in Britain. At the moment it is too often an efficient means of facilitating foreign imports. This is against the long-run interests of British retailers; for if British industry is overwhelmed by imports, then incomes in Britain will grow very slowly, or even decline, taking demand down with them. That is hardly an environment in which retailers will thrive. An important task for the Labour government will be to mobilize the power of Britain's major retailing chains in the recovery strategy. The retailers have the experience and the skills which will greatly aid British industry to design and produce competitive products which will sell in Britain and around the world. And their buying strategies provide the platform for the investment in capacity, research and design which is necessary in modern industry.

SOCIAL OWNERSHIP

Government intervention in the economy does not take place only through the DTI and other ministries. Major parts of

117

Britain's economy are wholly or partly socially owned, not only the utilities like gas, water, electricity and telephone, but also four out of Britain's top ten exporters: BP, British Aerospace, British Steel and the Rover Group (BL).

Social ownership of the utilities, like electricity, gas and water, which are necessarily natural monopolies, is simply economic common sense – although Tory government policy defies such sanity. The justification for monopoly in utilities obviously does not mean that the *content* of social ownership cannot be improved. In particular, the monopolies must be far more responsive to the consumer than they have frequently been in the past, and in addition to improvements which they seek to make at national, shop counter and repair service level, there must be consistent policy by government, as a representative of all consumers, to raise standards.

But utilities are not just providers; they are investors and innovators too. A large part of Britain's economic future is tied up with the success of Britain's energy industries. The socially owned utilities, together with British Coal, are key components in the rational long-term exploitation of Britain's abundant energy resources, which, despite the decline in oil output, remain one of our economy's great strengths. This strength must not be wasted.

In the interest of a rational long-term industrial policy, British Telecom must also be socially owned. The Tories' cut-price sell-off of BT has endangered Britain's future development in information technology, the industry which everyone knows is the key to our future economic wellbeing. We must have an integrated IT policy, with the research and development expertise and the buying power of BT at its core. Regulation of a private company won't do, since it mainly means supervision of the present rather than development in the future. And in IT the future is of paramount importance.

Since the government still owns 49 per cent of BT it has effective control of the company. This the Labour government will exercise. At a second stage Labour will bring BT back into full social ownership by acquiring all the equity. The Labour Party is well aware that many people have invested in BT, mainly in small shares or indirectly through institutions, and that these investors have an interest in the company. We will ensure that shares can be exchanged for non-voting securities that provide benefit from investment. These securities will be fully market-able, as are the non-voting securities issued by other companies, so the shareholders' investment will be protected in the same way as their equity investment is protected. Those people who have no long-term commitment to BT and wish to cash in their shares will be able to sell them to the government for 130p in cash, the price at flotation. It is worth noting, meanwhile, that the sell-off of 51 per cent of BT shares has hardly been the 'people's capitalism' that was advertised. The number of share-holders when the shares were issued in 1984 was 2.5 million, none of whom held more than 800 shares. The number has now fallen to 1.7 million and while blocks of 800 or less shares now account for 15 per cent of total share ownership, the top 800 shareholders – one half of one per cent – now own 78 per cent of private shareholdings. Shares held by BT workers, meanwhile, constitute less than 2 per cent of total shareholdings. BT is, of course, a highly profitable enterprise. In 1985, its first full year after privatization, the corporation made a profit on operations of £1,875 million. Instead of that being a public profit as pre-vious profits were, half of it – £934 million gross of tax – went to the shareholders.

In short, the sale of BT, while not adding anything to the productive or service strength of the corporation, has lost revenue for the great majority of the British people and failed to inhibit price increases. There could be no better example of the way in which the current government combines fanatical enthusiasm for denationalization and desperate desire to secure temporary funds for its programme with contempt for industrial needs and the public interest.

Labour will use social ownership as a means of pursuing national industrial policy, and bringing BT back into social ownership obviously makes sense for that purpose. As regards the other firms which were owned by the British people and have been sold off by the Tories, we have to assess them in terms of the goals of the policy. There are various options: a return to full social ownership, a stake by British Enterprise or involvement by the British Investment Bank. The extent, form and content of social ownership is flexible, but will include strategic shares in the defence and other key industries. The crucial point is that the option chosen must be workable in terms of our objective of improving trade performance.

A LONG-RUN STRATEGY

The theme which runs through all Labour's industrial policy is the need for a long-run perspective within which the industrial strategy can be worked out and put into effect. Previous attempts at pursuing a consistent industrial strategy in Britain have tended to fall foul of short-term economic crises which have resulted in the imposition of spending restrictions on the economy as a whole and on industrial projects in particular. It's easy to see the attraction of cutting industrial projects – it avoids the need to cut consumption or social expenditures. Yet in the long run such cuts are profoundly damaging, as we in Britain know to our cost.

It must be the responsibility of the Treasury to manage the short-run circumstances of the economy, and it is inevitable that the short run imposes itself – a crisis, no matter how transitory, must be dealt with *straight away*. That raises the problem of ensuring that industrial policy is conducted on the necessary long-run basis, and is not bundled out of the way by the vagaries of short-run management which are one of the Treasury's main concerns – even when the Treasury is led, as it will be under a Labour government, by ministers who are strongly conscious of, and committed to, the medium-term and long-run consistency of industrial policy.

Without the institutional structure and the policy conventions

120

prevalent in other countries, it would be difficult to safeguard that consistency. However, the need to maintain continuity for the sake of sustained development and the accumulating industrial strength which is vital for survival means that particular steps must be taken to prevent industrial strategy from being overwhelmed by Treasury tactical responses. The budget for the DTI and associated organs of industrial policy should be established early on and *separately* from the rest of government expenditure, and it should be adhered to. There is no danger that such an arrangement would inoculate either government providers or industrial gainers from the realities. They operate and will continue to operate in the real world and will be subject to its pressures. It is that very reality which requires the policy of industrial stimulus and support to persist, for without it those pressures will crush even more industries, and the people who work in and depend upon them.

It is consistent with that need to adopt changes in convention to make other re-arrangements in the respective roles of the Treasury and the Industry Department. Responsibilities for forecasting and statistical presentation are now, for instance, scattered among several Departments but the most crucial activities are confined to the Treasury. The exercise should be broadened to include other Departments at all stages and naturally the Industry Ministry would then have a direct participation. Such a change, while not diminishing the necessary authority of the Treasury as a Finance and Economic Ministry, would improve the calculation process and bring other Departments whose objectives and options are necessarily related to those of the Treasury closer into the process of decision making which the Treasury now dominates.

**INDUSTRIAL POLICY IN THE ECONOMIC REGIONS
OF BRITAIN**

In the course of – and partly as the result of – the industrial policy famine of the Thatcher years there have been new

121

initiatives and some advances in industrial policy making and application in places and institutions that were ideologically and often geographically miles away from the government. The Scottish and Welsh Development Agencies have done better than merely surviving and the local and regional enterprise agencies have developed a distinctive and mainly successful role in fostering and frequently founding industrial growth.

The enterprise boards were regarded with enormous scepticism when they were first established. How could boards run by local authorities swim against the tide of national anti-industry policy? What in the name of Mammon did local authorities know about industry anyway? Now, four to five years after boards such as the West Midlands Enterprise Board, The West Yorkshire Enterprise Board, Lancashire Enterprise Ltd and the Greater London Enterprise Board were established in the early eighties, they are widely acknowledged to have been successful. The enterprise boards have not only proved very efficient in their main objective of job creation, with average cost per job created being significantly below that of central government projects, but they have also proved to be effective catalysts of enterprise, offering technical and managerial advice, helping in the establishment of co-operative enterprises, organizing training and providing technological assistance.

The local enterprise idea works because it involves the community in planning its economic future. This involvement not only fosters commitment and practical partnership, it improves the local business environment and relationships among the local political, trade union and commercial interests to the benefit of all; and it plainly produces value for money.

The progress which has taken place, producing profits for ratepayers as well as jobs and sales, has all had to be achieved against a background of general economic depression and in the teeth of government clumsiness if not outright hostility. In improved economic circumstances and with deliberate encouragement from a government wishing to increase production and jobs these initiatives must certainly grow.

The regional development agencies in Scotland and Wales have also chalked up achievements. The development agencies have managed to combine financial and managerial initiative with a close involvement with regional planning authorities in Wales and Scotland. This relationship between each development agencies and local government has been an important element in success, as it has in the case of the enterprise boards. The extension of the regional development agency arrangements to the regions of England clearly requires that a similar structure of operational relationships is established.

These local and regional agencies must be fostered and expanded, local authorities must be enabled to develop local industrialization initiatives and people in small businesses must be provided with help in navigating through the requirements of bureaucracy. And on the basis of their record and their relationship with real conditions at the 'sharp end' of the economy those agencies must have access in terms of advice and influence at national level.

TECHNOLOGY POLICY

A major area of industrial policy which does not fit neatly into the DTI–NEDO planning framework is our policy on research and development, technology and design. The modernization of British industry is vital to its future success. Our industry is now in many areas so backward that we should be able to perform the Japanese trick of the fifties of copying ourselves to competitiveness. But we must also learn how to perform the Japanese trick of the sixties, seventies and eighties of innovating ourselves into a lead which can be sustained. Technology policy has numerous facets, from pure research in the universities, polytechnics and research institutes to the problem of disseminating throughout British industry new production ideas that work in practice.

Since 1967 expenditure on research and development in Britain has grown at a rate of less than 1 per cent per year. In

West Germany and in France it has grown at 6 per cent a year from a higher starting point. And whereas Germany devotes only 4 per cent of its research resources to military purposes, 27 per cent of our limited resources (and 54 per cent of government research and development funds) disappear into the military maw. It used to be argued that spin-off from military R & D would prove commercially viable in that it would promote other industries as well as arms sales, but even the beneficiaries would not argue that this has proved to be the case to any significant degree – certainly not to the point where it justified the absorption of sophisticated skills and huge sums of precious money. The problem is not only that military R & D is often too specific, and dedicated, in any case, to destruction; it is also that the 'leading edge' results are often classified as secret and therefore not available for commercial exploitation.

Unless we significantly expand our research and development effort and switch highly skilled researchers to commercially viable projects, we stand little real chance of competing in today's technologically sophisticated markets. It is essential that in Britain, as in other countries, government and industry must work in concert to achieve the best balance between applied research and development and pure research, and in the course of that given high priority to the objective of practical commercial outcomes. That this is now a matter of industrial survival is well known to people in the scientific community. The government must therefore fulfil the role of enabler, providing new facilities for funding, for co-ordination and for the use of R & D facilities, and do it in such a way as to retain the benefits of British developments in Britain, and ensure that the ideas are spread and used in large and small enterprises in the public and private sectors.

Small and medium-sized firms play a significant part in research, development and design today. The contrast between the large number of excellent internationally employed engineering research and design consultancies we have in this country, and the relatively weak state of many parts of British engineering industries, has a significance all of its own. The structural fact of life about many new technologies is that they come from small, specialist enterprises and they often need to be customized to meet specialist needs. Frequently, therefore, the need is for relatively small units with access to relatively big money over a relatively long term. The reality that small is not so much beautiful as just plain necessary has to be taken into account in a strategy to maximize the use of scientific prowess in the pursuit of manufacturing success.

In an environment of tough competition, a coherent strategy for science and its industrial use in Britain is more necessary than ever. The next Labour government will therefore form a new co-ordinating Ministry of Science which, without imposing impractical rigidity, will give the developer and the user in laboratory and industry a focus for reference, for representation and for two-way advice. The new ministry would also permit both a cogent view of public sponsorship and purchase of science and technology and more effective budgeting.

The programmes of the Ministry of Science must be carefully co-ordinated with those of the DTI and related to the work of NEDO. By that means, and acting on the basis of scientific and industrial advice, the industrial strategy can have the vital benefit of consistent and authoritative scientific and technological support.

Within industry itself there must be encouragement for more joint research among companies. The label 'pre-competitive' which has been attached to the activities of research clubs and similar collective activities has, it appears, proved off-putting to those companies who think that there is no such thing. What needs to be done is to establish suitable collaborative agreements with clearly defined rules for the distribution of the returns. This will require some amendment of the restrictive practices legislation, but this will be in the interest of the better fulfilment of the prime objectives of industrial policy, especially since it will promote the understanding of the

125

research clubs and those activities which necessarily precede specific industrial uses and adaptations.

LABOUR'S INDUSTRIAL POLICY IN ACTION

Two of the major industrial tasks facing the next Labour government will be to reverse the huge deterioration which has taken place in the trade balance in cars and in electronics and information technology. In both cases, the long-run competitiveness of British industry is at stake – not just in these two industries themselves, but in all the other many industries with which they are connected as purchasers, suppliers and providers of technologies.

The car industry

In the car industry three basic problems must be solved.

- First, the recovery of Britain's only mass vehicle producer, Rover Group, must be reinforced and enhanced.
- Secondly, the government must, through its trade policies, address the problem of the trade performance of Ford, GM and Peugeot–Talbot.
- Thirdly, we must ensure that technologically the industry as a whole is moving into the forefront of world motor industries.

And by the forefront I mean the forefront. It will not be enough to settle for second place in the European or even the world technology races. Unless we achieve technological parity we will not be able to start the long march back to the sort of market share we had even 15 years ago.

The Rover Group has not sought funds from the government for the past four years, and its progress has been clear to all. Nonetheless, the company has been continually impeded by an openly hostile Tory government whose destabilizing tactics have done the company enormous damage. The Labour government will support Rover Group. This does not mean that the government will be turning on a money tap for the company. There is no such tap; and under current circumstances anyway it is highly unlikely that the company would want us to do so.

Being in favour of a British company does not mean that we are opposed to Ford, GM and Peugeot–Talbot. We want them to succeed as employers and traders – but in terms of our national economy as well as in terms of their corporate success. The trade performance of these companies, their switch to substantial foreign sourcing, has been very damaging to Britain, and the trend must be reversed. We will want companies operating here to operate a 'good neighbours' policy. That means helping to fulfil our trade objectives by, for instance, preserving and enhancing the research and development work in Britain, improving and expanding the training that is done in Britain and steadily improving their trend trade performance. Since the companies value their activities in Britain and would clearly stand to gain in a growing, vigorous British economy it is necessary to impress upon them that the deterioration in the economy and in their markets that would be consequent upon a failure to improve their trade trend cannot be in their interests any more than it would be in Britain's interests.

The need for technological development, and for design development, is very clear in the motor industry. We must mobilize the very considerable skills which exist in Britain to maximize benefit *for* Britain. Rover Group has led the way in research and development relations with universities. We must also explore and develop the possibilities of cross-industry research collaboration. After all, many of the techniques being used in aerospace, for instance, are now used in the motor industry too, or soon will be, and there are clear benefits in collaboration in and adaptation of suitable technologies.

Information technology: the IT industry

Our approach to the needs and challenges in information technology will be broadly the same. We have catching up to do, but we do have the advantage of British Telecom as the centre around which to build the vital telecommunications dimension of the industry. We must develop an integrated approach, using an expanded and less academic Alvey programme to push into the future and the increasing strength of ICL to re-establish a significant presence in mainframe technology. We also need to examine the future of micro-computer technology and make sure that Britain is not squeezed out so ignominiously again.

Also, closer links must be established between the British IT industry and end users. We must encourage more commercial applications of computer technology by extending IT advisory services and investing in more process technology.

And in IT, as in the motor industry, the government must deal with major multinationals, IBM being the most prominent. Once again, for the mixed reasons of the national interests of Britain and the self-interest of the corporation, we will require 'good neighbourliness' in the form of a sustained trend improvement in the trade balance arising from the company's activities.

The Tories' policy toward IT has been slow-footed and half-hearted. They have found the obvious need for public investment ideologically distasteful, and so have wavered indecisively, attempting to hive off their responsibility on to an inadequate private sector, or even onto the European *Esprit* programme. Labour, while playing a full role in the European programme, will regard the development of Britain's IT capacity as a top priority of government in partnership with industry. That's how others have succeeded, and it is how we have to succeed too.

AN INDUSTRIAL FUTURE

Industrial recovery will be difficult. But we do face some new opportunities, if we can grasp them.

In the changing pattern of industrial development there is a discernible trend toward capital intensity, which is becoming more important than 'cheap labour' and even geographical advantage as the key determinants of industrial location. Investment in automation has in many industries reduced labour costs to less than 10 per cent of total manufacturing costs. This suggests that a new technological wave is changing the determinants of location as they have been established since the fifties. It would be unwise to found all hopes and strategies on such a thesis. But the possibilities do bear much more extensive examination.

If indeed there is a long-term industrial shift, it would mean that Britain, having missed too much of the industrial and technological tide in the fifties, sixties and seventies, could lock into a new movement for the eighties and beyond, without having to go through the intervening transition. There have been frequent occasions in the last 30 years on which industrialists, politicians and academics have reflected ruefully on the good fortune of 'new economies' in not having to repeat the mistakes of the 'old economies', and making their start at the latest high point of development. Without even supposing that it is possible for us to hitch an easy ride, it is not inconceivable that we could, if we are sufficiently vigilant and responsive, gain a 'new' economic advantage.

The principles which I have outlined above will guide the formation of a comprehensive, aggressive industrial policy, formulated with the direct purpose of achieving the resilient long-term modernization and recovery of the British economy. The policy measures and institutional structures which I have outlined follow directly from those principles.

Industrial policy will take a leading part in the formation of economic policy by a Labour government. The other components of economic policy have to fit the needs of industry, *not the other way around*. I will deal with the implications which this will have for taxation, monetary policy, and international relations in chapter 7. But before doing that I must turn to what is perhaps the most important of all the components of Labour's industrial policy: investment in people – education and training.

6
Education and Training

Education is today the principal route for individual advancement and national progress. In the post-oil era, as Britain moves towards a knowledge-based economy, education and training will become the key to future wealth creation. Parents, teachers, employers, the general public and, most particularly, young people recognize that. And they realize, too, that there must be a change in the financing and philosophy of education and training if this country is to be fit for the future as an industrially competitive, culturally vital, and just society.

Three considerations underscore our present sense of urgency. First, the future prosperity of the country will depend upon Britain's ability to develop and exploit new technologies, not only in the high-tech industries of the future, but also in the established manufacturing industries; yet the country is weakened by crucial shortages in a number of leading areas, such as information technology and engineering. Second, the lack of skilled workers is a central structural and historical weakness of the British economy and there is increasing evidence that the level of skills in manufacturing is critical to producing goods of the quality and sophistication demanded in international markets. Third, the country faces a crisis in youth unemployment of unprecedented dimensions. One in five young people under 25 and only 68 per cent of those between 20 and 24 are in work or in training at a time when employment opportunities for skilled and semi-skilled workers are vanishing and when the industries of the future will demand an even higher degree of technical and cultural competence.

In our long-term strategy for economic recovery, we cannot afford to waste any skills or talents. For economic efficiency, as much as for social justice, a clear strategy for education and training must be an integral part of our economic and industrial policy.

Finding a route to educational reform which matches industrial requirements does not mean that this will become the single purpose of education. Far from it. But it does mean that we must make a major investment of money that gives proper regard to designing, inventing, making and selling things. And, if our education and training service, which has the major responsibility for managing change, is to do this effectively, it must move into the future tense, and address four problems simultaneously.

It must be recognized that:

- A substantial and resilient commercial recovery will depend at least as much upon the trained abilities of the workforce as upon the availability of investment finance.
- The pace and diversity of technological change requires the constant updating of skills – among technologists, technicians and managers – and access to facilities for continuous learning and re-learning.
- The destruction and creation of occupations which accompanies technological, administrative and social change demands facilities for moves within and between occupations.
- New patterns of employment will bring with them an increase in the time spent outside the workforce: this requires our education system to encourage 'life-skills' to facilitate and sustain the creative and fulfilling use of leisure.

These are large demands to place on an education system which in the past has, despite the efforts of teachers and the demands of pupils, parents and employers, been geared to providing specialist academic qualifications for a minority of each generation.

In order to meet the demands and speed of economic, technological and social change, this system will have to tackle four broad problems:

- the need for general improvement in the effectiveness of education at all levels for children of all abilities and levels of achievement;
- the production of more and better scientists and technologists for all types of careers;
- the creation of a better trained and more technologically literate workforce;
- the provision of a curriculum that is broad enough, and an opportunity for continuing in education that is long enough, to provide young people and adults with the learning necessary to deal with the complexities and changes facing them inside and outside work.

The question is not whether this can be done. It must be done. The question is what is the most effective strategy to adopt.

WHERE DID WE GO WRONG?

There are many diagnoses (some cultural, some economic, some political) of the failure of the British education system to provide the necessary stimulation and support for the economy. Many are familiar to the point of cliché. But, like all clichés, they contain a truth.

It is a cliché, for example, that the inadequacy and long-term decline of British manufacturing industry is a result of a cultural hostility towards industry, and towards the 'practical man' and the engineer, that originated in the Victorian public schools and older universities. These institutions elevated the classicist at the expense of the technologist, the 'pure' academic – including the pure scientist – at the expense of the practical innovator, and the administrator at the expense of the specialist. The disdain of the public school educated son of the Victorian entrepreneur for industry thrust him into the realms of the Civil Service and the professions. Today, his descendants have joined the ranks of bankers and investment advisers, the ad-men and the insurance fraternity. To be 'educated' is still to be something or somebody in the City, the law, medicine, higher education or the media.

Despite efforts from the teaching profession the school curriculum continues to be dominated by the examination requirements of a handful of academically oriented young people destined for higher education. Enforced specialization at an early and impressionable age deters potential scientists and engineers – particularly women – and condemns both boys and girls to a career path where second chances are exotically rare. Technical competence and personal skills are still too often designated as 'vocational' and therefore considered to be in some way inferior to 'academic abilities'.

Many deficiencies of the orthodox British curriculum have deep and stubborn roots. Between 1850 and 1900, as four Royal Commissions pointed out, a much smaller proportion of the British population was educated in scientific and technical subjects than was the case in Germany. By 1939, despite the piecemeal reorganization and expansion of education, the UK still lagged well behind. The 1944 Education Act was designed to create a 'separate but equal' status between grammar, secondary modern and technical school systems. For the first time, the education system attempted to provide appropriate, stimulating and useful education for the 80 per cent of pupils thought to be 'non-academic' and, as a by-product, to provide the technically able workforce required by British industry.

This brave new world did not materialize. Few technical schools were built; no public examinations were created for the secondary modern schools; and part-time continuation schools were not created. Over the next 30 years 'separate but equal' provision in education never brought parity of esteem. It came to mean the prestigious award of 'O' levels for the academic and, in time, the limited value of the CSE for the rest. Where resources were made available they were diverted, not to further or continuing education, but to higher education, where, in the creation of a binary policy separating polytechnics from universities, a new distinction of status was established. It is significant that Britain has been unique among the major industrial European countries in the extent of the neglect of the majority of its young people as they move from school to adult life.

The structural weaknesses which have been noted since the end of the last century find an echo in successive recent warnings from our own contemporary authorities. the Cockroft Report on Mathematics, the Finniston Report on Engineering, the Royal Society Report on Science Education, the successive reports of the NEDC, and the House of Commons Reports on Education and Training for New Technologies, and Employment, together with the House of Lords Report on Overseas Trade, all clarify and confirm the same set of interlocking problems.

Time and again, apart from the general question of functional competence, Britain is shown to be deficient in four crucial and significant ways by comparison with our major competitors:

- Fewer young people stay on in school or go on to further education in order to secure additional qualifications;
- the academic bias of the curriculum deters and diverts young people away from vocational and technical skills;
- Britain simply produces too few scientists and engineers, and the problem is self-perpetuating;
- 'training' for work, or in work, is seen as an expensive encumbrance by the majority of employers, and has been chronically underprovided by government.

These are serious and authoritative criticisms. They reflect not only upon the history of education and training, but also

135

upon a complex of industrial attitudes towards long-term investment in technical training, research and development, and the
employment of scientists and technologists, which have been a
serious handicap to industrial innovation and development for
many years.

It is only in Britain, for example, that it is expected that the
majority of 16-year-olds should try to enter the labour market
directly at 16. In Japan only 5 per cent do so; the vast majority
stay on in school until they are 18, raising the levels of numeracy, literacy and comprehension before leaving school. In the
United States, most young people take a High School diploma.
In Britain, only 31 per cent of all 16-year-olds stay on in school;
and this figure is itself subject to wide regional and class
variations.

With regard to vocational education, the comparison with
West Germany is only too familiar. In West Germany, vocational education in the last years in school has been of immense
importance in the creation of a skilled workforce. But this is
combined with two other factors: a measurably higher standard
of basic skills, particularly in mathematics for those at the lower
end of the ability range, and a comprehensive apprenticeship
system in craft skills which is regulated and monitored by
government with the full participation and support of employers.

In Britain, on the other hand, the failure of the technical school
idea has meant that until very recently, with the introduction of
the Technical and Vocational Education Initiative (TVEI),
technical education was relegated either to the 'failures' of the
secondary modern or the margins of the comprehensive schools.
TVEI, introduced from outside the education service, grafted
onto the syllabus by way of pilot projects, is the first attempt to
systematize provision.

The other significant characteristic of British education is
enforced specialization at too early an age. One result is that we
simply produce too few scientists and engineers. The Finniston
Report described the 'vicious circle' of prospects whereby the

narrowness of the choices open within the specialized curriculum enforces choices which are immature, underinformed and speculative. The effect is generally disadvantageous, but it is especially deterrent to girls who have proved notoriously reluctant to seek qualifications and careers in science and particularly engineering. In engineering departments in British universities, there are almost no women staff, and only 9 per cent of students are women. The situation becomes even worse further up the ladder. Among professors or research directors, or Fellows of the Royal Society, women virtually disappear from view. The whole process reinforces the banal orthodoxy that girls are not 'interested' in science and the even more superstitious nonsense that girls are not 'capable' in science. Both have the effect of persuading many girls and not a few parents and teachers that science, technology, engineering are somehow 'not for them'. The whole attitude is mediæval. For the individual it means the neglect of abilities, for our society and economy as a whole a loss of talent which we cannot afford. Other countries which have proportionately many more women scientists and engineers do not make the same mistake. They do not waste their womanpower so prodigiously. Neither must we.

Other Western industrial societies also give a far higher status to the engineer. It is only in Britain that the engineer is still seen as a superior technician. Although the attitude is gradually changing it will, at the present rate of progress, be a long time before the engineer with qualifications at degree or equivalent level is generally perceived to have parity with other graduate professions. Comparison by numbers is again instructive. In Germany, 53,000 students began engineering courses in 1983. In Japan, where between 100,000 and 150,000 engineering graduates are produced each year, they form 40 per cent of all graduates and, as the NEDC Report, *Competence and Competition*, puts it: 'the Japanese education system provides and Japanese industry uses, the engineering skills necessary for an advanced industrial nation in abundant quantities whilst the education system and industry in the UK do not.'

137

Finally, there is another hurdle to be overcome in the form of the attitude of industry itself to training. A recent report by Coopers and Lybrand on industrial attitudes towards training is only the latest confirmation of long-standing experience. Few employers, said the Report, 'think that training is sufficiently central to their business for it to be a main component in their corporate strategy; the great majority did not see it as an issue of great importance . . .'. Compare this complacency with the situation in Germany where there is a strong and systematic tradition of training, based on legislation, monitored for quality of content, producing recognized and transferable qualifications and guaranteed by approved employers; or with France, where legislation specifies minimum expenditure by employers; or even with the United States, where there is a strong voluntary emphasis on training as part of the entrepreneurial experience.

DEPRIVING OUR FUTURE

Given the consistency and urgency of the warnings on all sides that something must be done to prevent further national deterioration, it is all the more perverse that the policies of this government seem designed to accelerate that decline. The recent flurry of activity in relation to examination reform and vocational education and training is little more than damage-limitation – underfunded reactive measures which neglect the structural weaknesses within the education system. Moreover, they can hardly compensate for (indeed, are seriously undermined by) public expenditure policies which over the past seven years have robbed education of £1,000 million and which, apart from some cosmetic pre-election provision for secondary schooling, are set to continue in primary, further, higher and adult education.

The fact is that under this government education, and the opportunities of those who depend upon it, have slowly and relentlessly shrivelled. The percentage of GDP now spent on

138

education is less than it was in 1979, with real resources cut by 59 per cent. Parents now contribute an estimated £40 million a year to the costs of *essential* teaching and learning materials. Free schooling has been seriously eroded and in many areas – as Her Majesty's Inspectors', teachers' and parents' reports testify – the quality of provision now depends substantially on the contributions of parents.

Year after year Her Majesty's Inspectorate has reported the growing disparity between what the schools are required to do, and what they are able to achieve. Year after year the connection between decaying buildings, inadequate supplies of textbooks and library books, shortages of materials and equipment for art and science, the loss of specialist and remedial teachers, the amputation of parts of the curriculum, the increase in mixed-age teaching and large primary classes, the loss of opportunities for in-service training, and the performance and satisfaction of both teachers and children, has been made abundantly clear.

The objectives of *choice, standards* and *relevance* must be central themes of education. They have been debased by the present government in order to mobilize prejudice, feed propaganda and provide excuses for narrowing and reducing provision – and therefore choice, standards and relevance – for the great majority of school children. The expansion of choice, the raising of performance standards, the increase of relevance, together with other objectives of education like social and cultural enlightenment, good behaviour, responsibility, self-confidence, the encouragement of the appetite for knowledge, the fulfilment of potential, the development of the individual regardless of sex, or race, or economic circumstances, are desirable. But they are only significant if they are supported and reinforced by adequate resources and implemented in a partnership with the professionals that can foster success. Choice is mocked as the pressures of shortages push another generation into the same old, narrow avenues, and when confrontation rather than co-operation informs relationships among government, teachers and education administrators.

In the midst of this vicious circle of underprovision, demoralization and inefficiency, the outlook is bleak. In Industry Year, 1986, the teaching profession, undervalued and badly demoralized by a prolonged dispute, is short of 600 physics teachers; an estimated 1,000 non-physicists are teaching physics, and applications for teacher training places are down. At the same time, trained young specialist teachers are leaving the profession in despair at the way in which the demands made upon them multiply while the resources they need diminish. These teacher shortages will, of course, reproduce themselves as fewer and fewer young people take up the options in mathematics, science and technology. In the crucial area of Information Technology the country will be short of 5,000 graduates in 1988 and there are certainly no adequate means currently available to upgrade the skills of existing workers in that area on anything like the scale and speed necessary.

When the impact of government policies on training is examined an equally alarming picture emerges. The traditional method of vocational education and training for the 16–19 age group – or, at least, boys in that age group – has been the apprenticeship. But during the last few years the numbers of apprentices starting in British industry has declined drastically, from 120,000 in 1979 to 40,000 in 1983; while in the latter year in Germany 620,000 young people were beginning high-quality apprenticeships. The decline in the number of apprenticeships has been due partly to the massive contraction of manufacturing industry and partly to cuts in government support for local government. Little of the reduction has come as a result of the modernization or reform of initial training. And while government economic policies were wiping out apprenticeship opportunities, the government was also closing Skillcentres, abolishing 16 Industry Training Boards and withdrawing Exchequer support for industrial training and retraining. Apologists for the government insist, of course, that the operations of the Manpower Services Commission and the Youth Training Scheme in particular are more than making up for these losses.

It is true that the efforts of people in the MSC, the YTS and the associated activities can produce training of high quality. But the scale of that standard of provision is simply not great enough to compensate for the losses, let alone meet modern training and retraining needs in a country where mass unemployment adds to the crises caused by a history of undertraining.

The apprenticeship system, the Training Boards, the Skill-centres all fell short of perfection. But they have not been replaced by a superior system meeting the comprehensive training needs of youngsters and adults or significantly improving the skill supply of the nation. They have been replaced by forms of mass provision which beautify the unemployment figures but too frequently fail to enhance either the employment prospects of individuals or the strength of the economy.

The YTS has the advantage that it is universal and, at long last, is being extended to two-year duration. But that extension, the facility for qualification, the opportunities for continuing education and the resources for instruction and for payment to trainees have been grudgingly granted. As a result, Tory politicians have not met the requirements identified by those experienced in education and training. The arguments of the latter should be heeded. They are not empire-building and they do not make the case for greater quality or quantity of support and improved programme content and opportunity out of selfishness. Rather, they recognize that half-hearted provision means downhearted trainees, incomplete and devalued training and, in many cases, a cynicism which overwhelms youthful and parental hopes.

Given the history of deficiency in British training and the division in attitudes and therefore expectations between 'education' and 'training' in our country, it was not surprising that the approach to change should be faltering, cautious and prone to the errors of snobbery, conservatism and complacency. In many ways, change on the scale that has been needed for decades would amount to a cultural, educational and industrial revolution against ignorance, short-sightedness, convention and vested interests. The decades have certainly passed; and some of the change has come – but slowly, and circumstances now require urgency. That urgency is simply not manifested by the government, and industry, with a few honourable exceptions, has neither the will nor the feeling of obligation to meet large-scale additional provision spontaneously.

Trained and educated human abilities, the incomparable requirement of resilient economic recovery and advance for the Britain of the 1990s and beyond are not being developed to anything like the extent necessary to meet national needs. The seed-corn is either being devoured, as education and training are cut or constrained, or not even being planted. The consequences for the harvest are clear and awful.

HIGHER EDUCATION AND RESEARCH

The catalogue of destruction, the sacrifice of long-term prosperity to short-term 'savings' is nowhere more grave in its implications for the country than in the attacks on higher education and research. Between 1981 and 1986 the universities' budget was cut overall by 16 per cent. Cuts totalling a further 10 per cent are planned for the next five years. Morale among scientists and university teachers has, according to the President of the British Association, never been lower.

Future government expenditure plans also mean that work funded by the Research Councils will diminish by more than 10 per cent during the remainder of this decade. The recent report of the Advisory Board of the Research Councils has shown that Britain spends less per head on science than Germany, the United States, Japan, France and the Netherlands, and that among the areas of research which are underfunded, and which will be of crucial significance to the industrial future of the country, are the application of computers in engineering, micro-electronics, and biotechnology and protein engineering.

142

On top of this, at least 10,000 places in higher education have been lost and thousands more qualified students will be turned away over the next few years unless present plans are changed. Three thousand university teachers have been made redundant, and the universities have been subjected to a campaign of harassment which has provoked a new brain drain of alarming proportions. At the very time when we should be investing in all the scientific talent we possess – as other countries wisely are – by backing basic strategic and applied research, universities are closing their doors to the scientific workers of the future, shutting or reducing departments, and neglecting research in areas vital to our future.

The newly formed pressure group, Save British Science, estimates that £100 million is needed now to ensure that the very best research is funded. In evidence to the House of Lords, they comment that the crisis points in British sciences are 'everywhere' and affect all ranks of scientists. 'Our conclusion' they say, 'is not only that damage has been done, but that some of it may already be irreversible. The lead even in technologically important areas of research has been allowed to slip to other countries.' On their evidence, substantiated by the experience of other professional bodies of scientists, the best young British scientists – in inorganic chemistry, virology, molecular genetics – are leaving. They are in despair at the lack of research funds, the reduction of research teams, the lack of research assistance and equipment and the lack of support from a government which talks of value for money and the importance of research – but which is destroying the sources of creativity and wealth for the future.

WHAT MUST BE DONE?

The task facing the next Labour government and the country, is, to say the least, formidable. It is more than the need for significant and effective investment in all branches of education and

143

training. It is the need to replace the present inefficient and divisive system with one which is appropriate, comprehensive and effective for the needs of the economy and society in the twenty-first century. We shall have to spend money in order to save it. We shall have to invest in order to produce. And we shall have to do this in the knowledge that there are competing and equally urgent calls for repair and replacement of the buildings, stocks, resources and staffing in all areas. But we cannot let the short-term emergencies, great though they will be, divert us from tackling our present weaknesses at source.

Adequate investment in primary and secondary education is the key to raising and extending achievement standards. However, the primary schools have a particular claim because they are literally *priming* schools that, next to parental influences and the general social, cultural and economic environment of the young child, are the greatest determinant of attitudes, enthusiasms and capabilities. Free of the confines of the eleven-plus examinations, most primary schools have been successful in improving both the levels of numeracy and literacy and much wider social and scholastic prowess. But still the classes are too big, the number of specialist teachers too small, and the support services for mother-tongue teaching and special needs too few.

Within the primary and secondary school curriculum, we need to put fresh emphasis on, and commit new resources to, language and written and oral communication. It is not merely a matter of functional literacy. It is a need for fluency and for discernment and confidence in generations who will give and receive communication through a wider variety of written, aural, televisual and computerized means, and have to deal with greater time for leisure, than any previous generations.

And it is in primary school that we must make technical and vocational subjects, as well as science, technology and computing, a familiar part of every child's learning experience. Taking advantage of the wealth of research into ways of making science accessible and interesting to the youngest child, we can prevent the hostility, bewilderment, and even fear which so

144

many girls and boys still, in the age of video games, feel towards science and mathematics, and their offspring like computing.

In the primary and secondary schools, as well as in post-school education, we must, in response to national economic need and to individual social and occupational requirements, fulfil new standards of provision in science teaching and learning.

Not only must more science and technology be taught at every level if we are to produce the scientific workers of the future; it must be better taught by more teachers who must themselves have the stimulus and the support of in-service training to update their knowledge and methods. The curriculum must be overhauled so that it enables young people not only to be part of economic change, but also to take advantage of it in a world where science and technology impose increasingly complex ethical and technical choices. The implications of nuclear power, the destruction of forests by acid rain, the exhaustion of mineral resources, the contamination of the environment, the impact of a new generation of computers – all these developments will affect our lives. We have a moral obligation to ensure, as far as is possible, that our children as adults can make decisions based on the fullest information and most judicious choice. This requires a general science curriculum for everyone, in which science, and its applications to industrial, economic and social development, are taught in their widest context. In this way the activity of science can become less exclusive, less alienating, less mystifying, and ultimately more accountable to democratic control.

At the heart of the curriculum change is the science teacher, without whom all reforms are doomed. The immediate task is to address the problem of teacher shortages in mathematics, the sciences and craft, design and technology. The teaching profession must be made properly rewarding. The divisiveness of internal salary differentials based on subjects would only serve to demoralize the profession even further and ignore the needs of primary education. It would also devalue other subjects which

145

might not to be quite so chronically afflicted by shortages but which are nonetheless vital and still require people of specialist qualifications and professional commitment. The movement towards adequate standards of pay, the designation of a better teaching career structure and the proper recognition by government, in its dealings with the profession, of the role and commitment of teachers and of the need to improve the teaching and learning environment are fundamental to our strategy for necessary change. A new deal for teachers is essential; that means a better deal for pupils, but it must be strengthened by other policies to retain graduates and serving teachers in teaching science, and to provide more conversion courses to enable experienced teachers to follow new subject directions.

Our secondary schools aspire to ensure that no child leaves school without qualifications that are economically and socially useful to the individual. Teachers, pupils, parents and employers are not satisfied that the aspiration is fulfilled. There is a persistent and justifiable feeling amongst all of those groups that a system which has a statutory and universal obligation towards all children at the age of five has, by the time that those same children are 16, settled for sifting, not primarily as a means of diagnosing and guiding abilities and needs but as a means of doing the best in a limited and limiting system.

It is necessary to revise and extend the notion of what a qualification is and what it measures in a system of preparation and testing for qualifications. To meet modern requirements, the systems of certification and qualification should themselves stimulate higher levels of achievement among children at all levels of ability and aspiration. Examinations need to be diagnostic and give much greater significance to continuous and frequent assessment, placing less emphasis on single 'doomsday' testing. They should measure comprehension and application of knowledge rather than memory. They should test competence, in its widest sense – skills of communication, discernment and judgement – rather than just 'examinable knowledge'. They should encourage further effort and continued learning for

146

higher qualification rather than being a 'final hurdle' of school-ing. An examination system of that kind and the curriculum supporting it would be 'relevant', would produce real choices within subjects and schools and would raise standards of achievement by ensuring that abilities and lack of abilities were consistently identified and strengthened or stimulated. It wouldn't be cheap. Indeed, only the failure to do it would be more expensive.

The GCSE, the General Certificate of Secondary Education, is a step in the right direction, as are the introduction of pupil profiles and the extending use of the Technical and Business Education Certificates. But we need to go further, towards a system which allows for the accumulation of credit throughout education. We must develop curricula which are modular in character, which take building blocks of experience and study in each subject and which permit development according to apti-tude and ability. And, based on a modular approach, we must extend the principle of assessment throughout education. That would mean that all children have definite and attainable stan-dards to work for, know what they have achieved, and take away from school a record of effort and success rather than apathy and failure; a record which acts as a valid currency for further educational and training progress and an inducement to continue learning.

Education and training: 16–19 years

The seriousness with which we tackle the need for change will be measured in particular by what we provide for that most vulnerable and important age group between 16 and 19.

In recent years, with the catastrophic drop in apprenticeships, and the gradual and piecemeal development of the YTS, the quality of training has not risen to meet modern demand. With-out slavishly following, we must profit from the experience of Sweden, Spain, France and Germany. We have to recognize that the demarcation between education and training acts as a brake

147

on progress and that training cannot be left to the hope that enough employers will turn up. We need a national training programme that is a real partnership between public and private manufacturing and service employers, educational authorities, trade unions and training agencies.

In the 1982 Labour Party document, *Learning for Life*, we set out our plans for integrated provision, based on the premise that it should be designed, first, to get better value for learners (and for taxpayers) by breaking down the artificial barriers between education and training and allowing the education system to play its rightful part. Entitlement to that non-compulsory third or 'tertiary' stage in education, we argue, should be enacted as a right. And to make such a right meaningful, young people should be paid during their extended post-16 education and training – the 'earn to learn' principle. Secondly, the reform of education and certification must continue at this tertiary stage, permitting a combination of learning by tuition and learning by experience. It must offer opportunities of continuing to more advanced levels, of transfer between subjects and disciplines, of proper counselling and of qualifications that have validity for employers, universities and other institutions of Higher and Advanced Further Education and for the individuals themselves.

It is not only aspiring workers who must be trained, but workers already employed and unemployed workers. But the response of this government to new technological, economic, employment and demographic realities has been almost entirely confined to the operations of the centralized and separate Manpower Services Commission, which was conceived and staffed for much more limited purposes. The result is that the Commission, without any significant educational experience or standing, without obligation or accountability, has produced a Youth Training Scheme, now extended to a two-year span, which is still deficient. The extension of the one-year scheme for a second year without significant additional funding is indicative of the failure to provide a programme which is geared to real training rather than to cheap labour. The new scheme still offers no assurance of enhanced qualifications or dependable job opportunities; still imposes unfair burdens on underfinanced further education institutions; and still has unrealistic dependence on employers.

In order to provide training of the quantity and quality needed, employers, the unions, the MSC, the Education Service and the government must work together to establish and operate a more coherent approach towards the planning of all education and training provision from 16 years onwards. For young people, the range and quality of the YTS should be improved. The training workshops and community projects, many of which have been closed down, are valuable and deserve support. The quality of employer-based training schemes could be enhanced with additional time and resources for education and training, with improved Area Manpower Board procedures for monitoring and more support for careers advice, counselling and the training of trainers.

We also need to expand apprenticeships urgently in trades and occupations where skill bottlenecks have formed, and to reconsider the creation of Apprentice Training Centres, perhaps on the French Michelin model, where production experience is fully integrated with an extended full-time education programme leading to certification.

The provision of better quality training is not simply a job for the central state. Much of the impetus, by legislative and other means, and much of the resources must of course come from government. But to be really effective training provision should be related to regional and sectoral knowledge so that the design of courses, the setting of training standards and the determination of entrance requirements can be sensitive to the varying industrial and local realities.

The Industrial Training Boards have successfully pioneered these developments, and we must build on their experience. On this pattern, a programme geared to the needs of each major industry could be developed to determine, on the basis of full collaboration between unions and employers, and with expert assistance, what written or practical qualifications were appropriate, to determine the work content of training within companies, and the monitoring of training. Such a programme would in itself constitute a long-term plan for industrial training.

But in order to overcome the low priority given to training within industry, however, we must consider the options for new regulation and funding. In 1984, in *A Plan for Training*, the TUC and the Labour Party advocated a 'new right to training' which would mean placing a legal duty on employers to train all young workers to a required standard and to release them for on-the-job training without loss of pay. This legal duty must clearly be backed by resources, including training subsidies, or it will be yet another fine, free, and therefore stillborn idea. This policy, with the additional effort to ensure that employers develop and publish annual plans for training, will help to compensate for the short-term horizons which have for so long damaged the effectiveness of industrial training.

There is a particular responsibility upon the next government to develop retraining opportunities for adults. In *Education throughout Life* (1986) we have described a programme for comprehensive educational opportunities after 18 designed to remove those academic and financial barriers which prevent men and women from updating their skills or acquiring new vocational qualifications. Adults in work should, in order to meet modern realities of change within and between jobs, have the right to paid educational leave and assisted leave. Adults out of work must be given far more opportunities by way of training places, more skill centres and financial assistance for further and continuing education. Before the propaganda producers who pass for Treasury ministers in the Tory government start to hallucinate about immediate or even five-year public spending implications and imaginary tax borrowing requirements, I emphasize – as I always have – that all of those proposals, like much else in the programme of education and training reform we are formulating to improve our national productive performance, will take huge amounts of money and many years of time to implement fully. Even while recognizing that, however, it is impossible to evade the fact that if we are even to lay the foundations of an educational system that is capable of responding to rapid change and of forming the basis for economic advance we must, before the eighties are out, at least begin the programme of investment and reform as a strategy for survival as an industrial nation.

Education and research: the higher levels

Our strategy for education and training involves a clear commitment to increased funding for higher education. That is necessary to promote access to these opportunities which will generate that qualified manpower and womanpower that the country needs at all levels, to enhance the essential relationship between good teaching and active research in all disciplines, and to vitalize that basic and strategic research which, in partnership with industry, has to provide the tools, the products and the jobs for the next century.

It is clear that other strategies for development will be stifled if we cannot retain our best scientists and technologists, fund their work (including their efforts in the unpredictable but critical activity of basic research) and enable our universities, polytechnics and research councils to plan confidently and efficiently for the future. In our overall plans for investment and management of research and development, we will need to meet the *real* costs of science – not merely because we fear the loss of international prestige, but because we will prejudice our national economic survival if we do not. The relationships between science and technological development, among research, innovation and development, are subtle, complicated and often unavoidably speculative but we must find ways of state funding and management which will promote these relationships more effectively. Investment in research and development, whether within higher education, in government laboratories, in industry or in all three must be deliberate,

151

continuous and consistent if the technologies of the future are to be produced and diffused.

Education for industrial recovery

Education, training, research; all three must all be part of an explicit and co-ordinated strategy to ensure that the full talents of the people of this country can be liberated and mobilized. The national interest demands that we do so, despite the deep-seated problems which afflict our education system, despite the real difficulties in translating research into development, and then into economic success, and despite the traditional resistance of industry to long-term investment in training. I am confident that this strategy is necessary for our times – and that it can work. The principal reason for my optimism is that there is a clear mandate for change; a national sense of outrage not only at the conspicuous and appalling waste of unemployment, but also the waste of professional skills, commitment and competence. This mandate for change is the first precondition for action. The country needs no persuading of the necessity for investment in education, training or research. It requires only evidence of an intelligent way to do what needs to be done, and the will to do that.

The next Labour government will provide both.

7
Supporting Supply

Labour's economic policies will be built around industrial policy. But no industrial policy can hope to succeed in a depressed economy in which retrenchment rather than innovation is the major theme of corporate policy. An industrial policy will obviously work best if the economy as a whole is expanding, if real interest rates are low, if the exchange rate is such as to give domestic industry a competitive edge, and if all these are maintained with reasonable stability over at least the medium term. An unstable economy creates uncertainty and imposes considerable costs on industry. Thus, Labour's prime objective must be to maintain a steady rate of economic expansion, at as high a rate as it is possible to maintain over the medium term.

The Tories simply opted out of the responsibility of influencing the level of output and the rate of growth. Their belief in 'market forces' extends to the determination of the rate of growth of the economy. If that rate of growth is too low to ensure the full utilization of Britain's productive resources, then the blame for that obvious inefficiency is always laid elsewhere on someone or something that is inhibiting the smooth working of the omniscient market forces. That something is, according to the Tories, generally a trade union or, at least some established arrangement introduced by a former Conservative, Labour or Liberal – yes, they go back even that far – government to try to ameliorate the excesses of the market.

Labour will not opt out. Like so many pre-Thatcher governments, we consider that, in government, we have a responsibility to manage the overall level of demand, by whatever tools are appropriate, to ensure the highest possible sustainable level of output.

It is obvious that the main tools available to the government are its expenditure and the taxes it levies, its monetary policy, particularly its policies on the level of interest rates and the availability of credit, and its policy toward international trade. It is equally clear that the government's spending and taxing decisions have the greatest influence on the overall level of demand, that its monetary policy has influence on the division of national income (the level of interest rates has a major impact on company cash flow), that the exchange rate has influence on competitiveness and a considerable effect upon the rate of inflation, and that these three major elements are not independent of one another. The art of economic policy is to find the right mix to achieve the government's objectives.

Our objective is to support our industrial policy, to ensure that the competitiveness of British industry is raised to the greatest degree possible, and so to ensure the greatest long-run growth of employment. It is crucial to the fulfilment of this objective that the growth of the economy be as consistent, year on year, as it can be. If alternatives have to be specified, it would be better to aim for a slightly lower rate of growth of demand, and to *maintain* that rate continually while at the same time making a major effort on the supply side, rather than to dash for growth and see the effort – and the growth – halt in crisis.

GOVERNMENT SPENDING

One of the Tories' major efforts has been to convince the British people that government expenditure is an incubus, a brake on enterprise, a coddling feather bed in which indolence, dependence and, yes, even immorality have been conceived. State

154

expenditure, they insist, is a Bad Thing. The case against it is always lurid but rarely clear, though Tories – at least the ones who still support Mrs Thatcher – usually equate it with 'inefficiency' or 'inflation' or both.

Given the fact that nothing is much more inefficient than leaving vast amounts of resources expensively unemployed, and that all the Tory cuts have had no discernible effect on our rate of inflation *relative to everyone else's*, their case, to say the least, owes more to political propaganda than anything else. That is particularly true of Mrs Thatcher herself. She has increasingly adopted the tactic of saying that since public expenditure has to be paid by the public, pensions and benefits, public investment in construction, industry and education cannot be much improved because 'the taxpayer' cannot take the burden. Since her policies have raised the national tax burden as a proportion of the personal incomes from 37 per cent in 1979 to 44 per cent in 1986, she should be an authority on that. But that apart, the Prime Minister is clearly trying to make the divisive case that Britain is neatly split into people called 'taxpayers' who fund everything and other people called 'non-taxpayers' who take everything. Since we are all taxpayers from our first bag of sweets to our funeral bills, and benefit users even before becoming sweet-eaters, Mrs Thatcher's image of a Britain of taxpaying worker bees and benefit-taking drones is hardly reality. Indeed, it would be the nearest she ever comes to making a joke if repeated references to it did not manifest one of her famous 'convictions'. She is obviously aware of the realities of taxpaying. She must be. But instinctively her terms of reference are that taxpaying is such a weight that it could and should be reduced if it wasn't for the lotus-eating pensioners and children and sick and ill-housed and unemployed and scientists and managers and building firms and civil servants lounging around waiting for handouts.

The British people are fortunately more adult. They don't much like paying taxes (who does?); but they would rather do that and meet the bills of care, opportunity, construction,

service and security than live in a country where those necessities are either absent, grossly insufficient or dependent upon
individual ability to buy them privately.

That being known, the Conservatives who still cling to the
Thatcherite case buttress their argument against public expenditure by comparing the share of British government expenditure in national output with that of other major industrial
countries, and relating that comparison to overall economic
performance. This exercise results in the discovery that government expenditure takes up a significantly smaller proportion of
national output in Japan and Germany, and they perform better
than we do. It also, however, produces the conclusive evidence
that government expenditure takes up a larger proportion of
national output in France, Italy, and Sweden, and that they
perform better than we do too. It has been argued that government expenditure 'crowds out' private expenditure, as if
resources in a modern economy were in a bag of a fixed size and
expenditure on public obligations tied up funds which would
otherwise be spent on *privately* sponsored growth. That is
clearly not the case. What is the case, however, is that in the
absence of adequate levels of private investment, adequate
levels of private expenditure, the state must step in to try to
make up for the deficiencies of the private sector.

If the private sector were investing in Britain, if demand were
being maintained at such a level as to ensure a decent rate of
growth of output and employment, then there would be no
reason to increase government expenditure on economic development just for the sake of it. In so far as the government
wanted to modify the structure of the economy, that could be
done by other means, ranging from varying taxes and subsidies
to taking firms into social ownership. But if sufficient expenditure is not forthcoming from the private sector then the alternatives for government are either to take action or to surrender to
decline. Today's Tories have done the latter, although they still
plaintively claim that private expenditure would automatically
adjust to the appropriate level if everyone else with a claim on

resources would only let it. Their hope could only ever have been fulfilled if the British people had been willing to tolerate even more swingeing cuts in every area of social and economic expenditure and somehow simultaneously able to sustain or increase levels of effective demand, the consumer spending necessary to make investment in production and sales worthwhile.

For seven years the government has been trying to cut overall government spending, both absolutely and as a proportion of GNP, and instead it has seen the totals rise to record levels. This has happened largely because of the ruinous effects of the cuts programme and its associated policy inanities on employment, demand and economic activity and the consequent massive rise in dole and poverty bills. After all that, the idea that public expenditure cuts will invoke a private investment rise, that Mrs Thatcher's 'get-up-and-go' economy can result from Mrs Thatcher's 'get-down-on-your-knees' policies is tragi-comic. Apart from the muddle of injustice, cost, waste and inefficiency which has resulted from those policies, the experience also shows that high public spending is clearly not, in itself, beneficial. High totals are no comfort if they are being spent on the wrong things or if they arise because of the poverty generated by other policies. Value for money and value for the people who pay it and spend it obviously depends on why it is spent and what it is spent on, as well as how much of it is spent. The amounts spent cannot simply respond to needs; they are infinite, resources are not. But it is stupid and cruel for a government to disable an economy or inflict unnecessary suffering on its people because of a fixation with totals that is so dogmatic that it actually results in achieving the opposite of its intentions, and so short-sighted that it vastly increases future bills of essential repair and renewal.

In a rearguard defence of their record the more desperate among Tory politicians are now playing a game of 'costing out' a Labour programme which they have invented. The aim of this gigantic Aunt Sally exercise is to show that 'the programme'

157

would involve levels of public expenditure which they predictably describe as excessive. Apart from the fact that these exercises are immensely exaggerated, dishonest and incompetent, they are also based on a serious conceptual error. No-one – certainly no political party with a prospect of power – would, or could, attempt to specify *precisely* what it plans to do in, say, its first two years in office, before it has had the opportunity in office to 'examine the books' and assess exactly what is possible. The important fact about Labour's programme is not just that we will spend more than the Tories, but that we have a different set of spending *priorities* from those of the Tories. Where their declared first – and singularly failed – priority is to cut taxes, our number one priority is to generate jobs and development. In that and many other respects our programme is *qualitatively* different from the sort of programme the Tories do pursue and would pursue further given the chance.

Given the present government's record of fiddling the statistics it would not be entirely surprising if we discover that they have made an even bigger mess of things than we anticipate at the moment. If that were the case then we would have to proceed more slowly than we at present intend. We will none the less still proceed – and in a direction that is quite different to that of the Tories.

We will implement the first stage of our recovery programme for Britain, the two-year emergency jobs programme, and with it we will begin the medium-term and longer-term strategies. We will implement the programme to transfer £3.6 billion from the best-off 5 per cent to the poor, since that is self-financing. We will also make changes in funding for health and education which are matters of national need and which, like initiatives in improving the environment and transport, are in themselves a means of providing jobs that need to be done for people who need to do them in a country that wants them to be done. The pace of advance in these areas is obviously dependent to some reasonable extent upon the resources that are available or can be made available at tolerable cost. The *direction* is not governed by that consideration. It is always towards recovery.

The speed of that development is, in this real world, obviously subject to the constraints on the rate at which we seek to stimulate demand as discussed in chapter 3, including the balance-of-payments constraint, and the rate of inflation. For even though the rate of inflation is not closely related to the level of activity in the economy or to the level of government expenditure, any significant rise in the rate of inflation will in itself set in train the events which I described earlier, and will force the government to proceed at a slower rate. All of the rationalizations in the world will not change that. The Thatcherite search for the Holy Grail of nil inflation has taken her policies trampling over industries, jobs, communities, services and people and still ensured that Britain has a high relative inflation rate and is subject, indeed *more* subject, to the vagaries of prices of international goods upon which we are much more dependent. But animosity to those policies should not obscure the advantages of containing inflation to the greatest possible extent.

DEALING WITH INFLATION

Inflation has been a perennial problem for Britain and for British economic policy. Three standard approaches have emerged: first, doing nothing; secondly, deflating the economy hard in the belief that a recession with high levels of unemployment will lead to a fall in inflation; and thirdly, imposing some form of general incomes control policy. All three, in practice, have failed to attack the real causes of inflation, that is, the attempt by various groups within society – companies, government, and workers – to maintain what they regard as a reasonable share of national income for themselves by bidding up their 'price', whether that price be profits, taxes, rents of various kinds or wage rates. If the economy is depressed, or the rate of growth is slow, or the prices of necessary imports have risen, absorbing more national income to buy them, then it may be that the demands of the various social groups for their share of the cake cannot be satisfied. There just is not enough to go round. In that case they will go on bidding against each other, forcing up costs, then prices, then taxes, then wages, then prices again in an accelerating spiral.

Dealing with inflation means dealing with the production and distribution of the national product. Typically, if more income goes to wages then consumption will tend to be higher than if a greater share goes to profits, a higher proportion of which are saved and not put into immediate consumption. A sensible framework within which to discuss the origins and consequences of inflation would, therefore, involve some assessment of how the national product is produced and how it is to be used. This is one of the important tasks of the National Economic Assessment which the Labour government will establish.

The National Economic Assessment stands at the core of the planning system. The distribution of resources among investment and consumption and various categories of government expenditure will be considered in the light of the objectives of the industrial policy. The negotiations will seek broad agreement upon the way in which the nation's resources are to be used for the purpose of promoting production and employment. This agreement clearly has to include understanding about the general level of incomes in the next year, for a decision about what consumption can be is a decision about what incomes can be. No-one who has subscribed to the National Economic Assessment policy believes that decisions about how much to invest and how rapidly to pursue the policy of industrial reconstruction can be separated from the decisions about the general level of incomes, for they are one and the same decision.

In the National Economic Assessment, therefore, government, management, and trades unions must strive to achieve agreement on investment and income, on costs of production and consumption, on incomes and on prices; for they are all part of the same whole. It is, of course, a revenues and rewards policy.

160

The very fact of government makes that necessary and no government has ever, or will ever, be able to govern without policies for both. Certainly, the current government has a rewards policy and it is the clumsiest, cruellest one that could be assembled; it consists primarily of mass unemployment and the fear of unemployment. But combined with that is its effort to destroy Wages Councils and all institutions and commitments to safeguard basic pay; its policy to cut the wages of those already low-paid in the public sector, by means of privatization and cash limits; and all this is topped off with statute law to inhibit the ability of trade unions to withstand these pressures on employees. As if that were not enough, it has a prices policy too. It consists of withdrawing £19,000 million of Rate Support Grant, so pushing up rates, rents and fares, and of allowing mortgage rates to rise to their highest level ever for the longest time ever. It depends upon actions such as a 1,000 per cent rise in prescription charges, reductions in Housing Benefit and the use of gas, electricity and water bills as a system of taxation.

That is the Tory (lower) incomes and (higher) prices policy. And everyone who has nothing to sell but their labour, everyone who must do that to make a decent home, raise a family, live a secure life, every worker – whatever their job or their income – should know it. They should also know that not a single part of that policy has come about by accident. The Tories did not impose their wage control or their price promotion policies because of some sudden economic crisis. They weren't 'blown off course'. This *is* their course and it has been from the beginning. Their whole economic policy relies – and always has relied – upon an increase in unemployment to impose discipline on the labour force. The policy towards the trades unions has been designed to reduce the unions' power to resist the effects of Tory slump economics. Their whole policy for public spending and public charging and all of their strategies for taxation, benefits and pensions have been aimed at, or have most certainly achieved, the purpose of shifting the burdens of payment from the richest in the community to the poorest in the community.

161

They call it the 'stand-on-your-own-feet society'; they say that it 'encourages independence from the state', that it 'makes people free'. The truth is the opposite. The result of their policies has been to depress and impoverish and intimidate. That makes people *less* free. More people are now dependent upon the state: unemployment has increased by millions; many thousands more have been pushed down on to wages that are so low that they qualify for rebates and Family Income Supplement; the numbers in poverty have doubled.

That, then, is the incomes and prices policy of the government that wasn't going to interfere or intervene, the government that was going to cut taxes, the government that came to power condemning prices and incomes policies.

Generating new employment is the task which is central to the policies of the Labour Party. The extra jobs will not come simply as additions bought by new government spending. While it is clear that some jobs will of course come from that and some will come directly as a result of the new economic climate, it is also obvious that some of the jobs and much of the future wealth to sustain recovery must come from the very success which can be achieved by industries and services in selling their products at home and abroad. If those sales are to be made, costs of production and rewards from production must be geared to that job of producing and selling our way to recovery. That is essential if the new resources that are needed to meet the social bills of better pensions, better training and better health and other services are to be generated, if the efforts against low pay are to be effective and if we are to have the means to make and keep jobs for men and women and for youngsters.

It is clear that much of the action necessary to get and keep production costs low must take place in relation to investment. And it is also obvious that policies to provide low-interest finance and to hold down the prices of household essentials are necessary components of any strategy for growth and must form the basis of agreement. Clear arrangements on taxes and benefits, dividends and incomes from capital are essential ingredients too, both for the purposes of advancing social justice and of using resources with maximum efficiency for the advantage of the British people.

And then there is the other component of costs and rewards: earned incomes, wages and salaries. For a tiny handful in our country they are too high. For millions they are too low. For almost everyone they are not enough – they never have been, they never will be. Faced with that situation, there are various options. It is possible to ignore it and hope that the problem will go away. It is possible to try to mobilize illusion, as the present government has, and seek to persuade people that the magic of the market will eventually give them everything they want. It is possible to wait for the tensions and panic to build up and engulf a government in bitter dissatisfaction. It is possible to try to pretend that there is no significance in the fact that for as long as governments have employed millions, fixed taxes, influenced prices and paid benefits, governments have had and always will have policies to determine their attitudes to rewards in their country.

All such options are worthless. It is better to face the fact squarely that by very definition governments do have policies for earning and spending. The consequent questions which arise, then, are not *whether* a Labour government will have such a policy; it goes with government, no more, no less. The real questions are:

- *Who* shall participate in making that policy?
- *What* will be its objectives and its priorities?
- *Which* groups will benefit or lose by awards or reductions or by tax advantages or increases?
- *How* will it be applied?

The process of resolving those questions within the National Economic Assessment will not be easy and it is unlikely to be smooth. But it will have to be done. And it can either be done there with agreement from the various representative parties

163

consistent with the objectives of employment, investment, trade, growth and social justice that have been specified elsewhere, or it will have to be done, albeit at a different, slower and less satisfactory pace, by the government, since no democratic government worthy of the name opts out of its obligations.

This is not a process of colonizing business or management, since its whole purpose is to develop an economic environment of growing demand and lower relative costs which will justify greater investment and generate sales. Nor is it a process that will weaken bargaining or try to replace local and workplace negotiation, since they are by definition diverse and intimate activities. Further, it is not a re-run of previous policies where the objectives and the rights and responsibilities have been vague and confused, since the rocks and reefs upon which those efforts have founded are all too obvious. It is not a repeat of the previous experience in which inflation was blamed uniquely on wages, controls were superimposed by law, and alarm in response to bankers' demands brought ill-fated attempts at pay policing policies. And it is certainly not related in any way to the policy of social and economic control produced by the unemployment of labour and capital which is practised and further *promised* by the Tory government.

It *is* very much an alternative to that system, a way of fighting low pay, a way of restoring and updating trades union rights and responsibilities, a way of getting a square deal for the young, the old and the sick, a way – the only way – of getting jobs, redressing injustice and reducing conflict.

Reality ensures, of course, that even the full operation of the National Economic Assessment would not mean that the problems of differentials would go away or that the agonies of comparability would be ended. But working for the agreement of unions and management to a practicable policy for contributions and rewards against the background of expansion, economic planning and improving social protection is an entirely different prospect from the policy attempts of the past.

The effort needed to achieve and sustain the necessary

consensus within the unavoidable constraints and the essential priorities will not be comfortable. But the chaos of a system in which companies contract and go bankrupt, union influence can only be exercised negatively, low pay is common and spreading, and poverty and unemployment grow is not recognizable as paradise either. And that condition has built-in deterioration. Worse begets worse.

THE BALANCE OF PAYMENTS

Relating the overall growth of unearned and earned income to the available resources is important not only because an excess growth of incomes results in cost and price rises but also because an important consequence of those rises is a deterioration in the balance of payments. Resources that are not available at home are bid in from abroad, the balance of payments moves into deficit, the exchange rate tends to fall, raising import prices and the rate of domestic inflation.

The prospect of a severe deterioration in the balance of payments is the fundamental determinant of how rapidly the economy can expand, how many people we can put back to work, and how soon and on what scale the major investments of the industrial policy can be made. I have indicated already that I do not see the lowering of the exchange rate as offering great or prolonged improvement to the balance of payments since the benefits of a price cut in our exports can be cancelled or offset by the rise in prices of necessary imports and, although valuable to some extent, the 'window of opportunity' between the two is limited. That is not to say that the exchange rate should be sustained at high levels for the sake of national 'virility'. The 'strong pound' has too often been a cause of economic weakness, especially when it is kept up by crippling interest rates. Our aim should be to shift the rate toward what is regarded as a reasonably competitive level and then hold it relatively steady in relation to the currencies of our major trading partners.

It has been suggested in many quarters that such stability could best be found by joining the Exchange Rate Mechanism (ERM) of the European Monetary System (EMS). Members of the ERM fix the rates of exchange between their currencies, and maintain those rates of exchange primarily by means of monetary policies (varying the rate of interest they offer to dealers on the international money markets in order to persuade them to hold their currency), and change the rate when under pressure after some negotiation with fellow ERM members.

For Britain, however, the fact is that as presently constituted the ERM would be not a support, but a straitjacket. The present stability of the ERM derives to a considerable extent from the fact it contains only one currency which is subject to major levels of dealing in the international money markets: the Deutschmark. If the pound sterling were added to the system then the presence of two currencies, linked at a fixed rate, would provide the opportunity for speculators to make huge one-way bets should one of the currencies come under stress. Then the only available mechanism to stabilize the system would be interest rates and massive currency purchases and the arrangement would leave us with either a very unstable currency or very unstable interest rates.

If the ERM were backed up with large, sophisticated packages of *mutual* currency support then it would be a different proposition. If, in other words, the various central banks agreed to act in concert to stabilize the system through credit and currency swap deals rather than interest rates variations, (and if European trade were organized on the more rational basis I outline below) then the ERM might provide Britain with some valuable stability in the foreign exchanges. But as it is, the ERM is not really suitable to Britain's needs. It will be better, therefore, to retain the degree of flexibility we have at present, together with the degree of uncertainty that the flexibility creates in the minds of the speculators.

If the exchange rate is relatively stable, the scope for expansion in the domestic economy will be determined by the following factors:

166

- First, our ability to finance any given rate of balance of payments deficit (the Americans are running a deficit of about $150 billion per year which they manage to finance by borrowing from other countries without, as yet, too much difficulty, at least for them).
- Secondly, the rate at which other economies, and the world economy generally, grow and create greater demands for our exports.
- Thirdly, the degree to which we can take measures to limit imports.
- Fourthly, the rate at which our industrial policy improves our competitiveness – a process which obviously offers no instant results.

Financing a deficit

The United States is at present running a balance-of-payments deficit of the order of 4 per cent of the gross national product. If we were to do the same the proportionate deficit would be about £13 billion per year. I don't think we would be able to do the same, and I don't think it would be desirable to do the same. The United States has a unique position at the centre of the monetary system of the West; its currency is used for most international transactions, which greatly enhances its ability to borrow funds from abroad. Britain is not in that position, and will therefore be able to sustain a deficit only at levels lower than those currently sustained by the United States.

There is nothing inherently 'wrong' with running a deficit that can be sustained, so long as the resources which are being sucked into the economy are being invested in the productive capacity which will earn foreign currency to pay off those borrowings in the future. The menace is, of course, that deficits result in a loss of confidence, a speculative run on the currency, and a financial crisis which leads to the expansion and the development programme being aborted. It is better therefore to run the economy at a lower rate of deficit than that which would

167

catapult the economy into short-term boom, than risk jeopardizing the long-run industrial policy. We can curse the irresponsibility, prejudice and power of the currency movers and rage against the instability which they threaten and the brake on progress which they impose. All of that is justifiable. It is also idle. And rather than have them cripple expansion it is better to develop productive strength and employment opportunities at a surer pace.

Fortunately, we can secure a valuable source of international finance to help pay for the industrial investment we need. The huge outflow of money which followed the Tory abolition of exchange controls in 1979 has resulted in a pool of dollar assets which, if repatriated to Britain, would cover balance-of-payments deficits to the tune of more than £25,000 million – well in excess of any deficit which we might contemplate. We will therefore encourage repatriation of funds by providing that those insurance companies and pension funds which hold more than 5 per cent of their assets in foreign currencies will lose the tax exemptions which they currently enjoy. As I noted in chapter 2, foreign holdings of insurance companies and pension funds have risen from roughly 5 per cent of their total assets in 1979 to roughly 15 per cent in 1986. Our regulation will encourage, though not compel, these companies to return to the situation which applied in 1979. If the funds do not return in part or whole we will, at very least, have the resources which could otherwise have been awarded as tax concessions. If, in part or whole, they do return, this country will clearly benefit from the additional investment resources. The people and concerns with interests in the insurance companies and pension funds do not, meanwhile, stand to lose by the scheme. The resources that are repatriated to this country will have rates of return comparable with those available elsewhere and, in addition, there will be the obvious and general benefit of a strengthened economy with an investment base that is firm and modern.

The money that was invested abroad after 1979 was essentially equivalent to that part of our earnings from the sale of oil which didn't go to cover the deficit on manufactures. Our scheme for encouraging the repatriation of foreign investments will do what should have been done in the first place – invest the earnings from oil in Britain – as well as discouraging future outflows. It should be noted that the loss of tax privileges we propose as a means of discouraging investment overseas and encouraging the repatriation of funds which have already been invested is far less restrictive than the regulations limiting foreign investments by French, Italian and Japanese pension funds. Nevertheless, we feel that it is appropriate to the British case. We will need to take a look too at the very high level of purely financial investment overseas being undertaken by commercial and industrial companies. Funding investments that for locational or commercial reasons are best made overseas is one thing. Exporting money that could and should be better used for production at home is another.

A GROWING WORLD ECONOMY

Britain's recovery programme would be much more easy to sustain, and the desired results achieved more quickly, in a growing world economy. If the industrial countries as a whole are expanding, then even relatively weak countries are pulled along with the rest.

The portents are not good. The world economy is today performing very badly. The United States' boom of the early eighties has run out of steam, and Germany and Japan are blamed for not growing more rapidly, taking up where the United States left off as an engine for world economic expansion. Policy by recrimination is no substitute for policy by negotiation and agreement. Indeed, policy by recrimination is really no policy at all.

We live in an economically interdependent world. And while that is obvious it does not lead inevitably to the action necessary to make that interdependence a source of mutual multilateral benefit and future trade and profit. It should. Indeed, if the world is not to wallow along in under-performance, debt, instability, famine and incipient crisis, it must. It is essential that the leading industrial nations construct an efficient international financial and trading system which takes account of the interdependence of countries and economies. By *efficient* I mean a system which facilitates sustained and resilient growth of material prosperity throughout the world and secures expanding employment in both the developed and the developing countries. These are the necessary foundations of individual opportunity, social progress and democracy, which itself is a by-product of economic health.

It is clear that the manner in which international trade and finance is conducted today is grossly *in*efficient. We only have to compare the condition in the years since the collapse of the old Bretton Woods system which used to regulate international trade, with the two decades which preceded the collapse.

In those 14 years

- the growth rate of world trade has been halved;
- the growth rate of output in the OECD countries has been halved;
- unemployment in the OECD countries has tripled to more than 30 million.

Of course, the international trading system as such is not solely to blame for this dismal record; the oil price shocks and the obsessive policies pursued by governments in the grip of monetarist ideology have played their part. But it is abundantly clear that the biggest economic threat facing us today is that from the persistent mismanagement of our international economic affairs.

Where in the world is the sense of a system in which Brazil and Mexico are forced by the IMF to impoverish their own people further in the name of 'sound money', at the same time deflating the demand for goods of everyone else? Where is the real profit in a system in which citizens of the richest industrial country on Earth seek desperately to raise protectionist barriers to cut imports, and so deflate world demand? Where is the sanity in a system in which any attempt to pursue full employment policies is regarded as financially 'irresponsible' and is aborted by pressure from the speculators, further deflating world demand? In such a system there might be avarice and meanness, but when the current and potential losses are so great it does not even have sincere materialism.

In our generation we have to find an alternative. And in that task we must have vision and common sense on the same scale as those who, tutored by two decades of slump and the ruinous World War that came out of them, gathered at Bretton Woods in 1944 in an effort to introduce order and mutual benefit to world financial and economic arrangements. Of course, we cannot go back precisely to the Bretton Woods system. The world has changed. But we do have to pursue much the same objectives by means which are not, in principle, very dissimilar.

As a step towards that we must sweep away some ideological nonsense. Consider, for example, Nigel Lawson's declaration in 1985 that 'our overriding aim' (overriding apparently *every* other economic objective) 'is to maintain a free trading and financial system at home and abroad. A free market system brings benefits for all. The more regulations we remove, the more barriers we can lower, the more liberal we can make our trading practices, the better off we shall be.'

It is, as a Tory of an earlier generation pointed out, by the illusions of such 'freedom' that peoples are enslaved. The very 'financial liberalization' which Lawson holds so dear has been a fundamental source of the instability which has depressed and distorted the world economy over the past decade. Just 18 years ago, in 1968, around 85 per cent of all foreign exchange transactions were for the finance of trade and long-term investment, and 15 per cent or so of the transactions were speculative. Today the situation is reversed – 85 per cent of all transactions in foreign exchange are for speculation and the devil takes the trading and investing hindmost. Financial liberalization and freely floating exchange rates have fed on each other to divorce movements in exchange rates and money from the realities of trade.

In this situation Nigel Lawson recommends 'selective intervention' to affect the 'psychology of the markets'. In the midst of the great and growing problems of unemployment, unstable exchange rates and high real interest rates, can anyone seriously make the economic destiny of the West so dependent on something as mystical, as intangible, as capricious as the 'psychology of the markets' – especially when those markets are so obviously detached from considerations of national and international manufacturing and trading needs?

On top of a free-for-all in the financial markets, Mr Lawson is also in favour of uninhibited so-called 'free' trade which, he declares, 'brings benefits for all'. This proposition is as superficial today as it was 100 years ago when the United States was surging toward industrial greatness behind the barrier of a 73 per cent tariff on the import of British manufactures. A serious case for the efficiency of free trade can, of course, be developed for a world in which trade is balanced, in which the participating countries are at similar levels of technical development, and in which all countries are operating at full employment. The problem is that none of these conditions apply outside the textbooks. Instead of laying the foundations for growing world trade, the disorganization and anarchy of the misnamed 'free' trade system form the source of creeping protectionism which endangers prosperity and the prospect of economic growth throughout the West. What we need, what we must have, is an internationally agreed framework in which trade is planned in the interests of growth and employment, and in which finance is the servant of trade, not its master.

The OECD countries are currently facing two pressing problems that an efficient international trading and financial system must solve.

First, the world system as currently organized has a built-in bias toward stagnation and unemployment. A country that tries to stimulate its growth rate will tend to suck in imports and soon acquire an unsustainable balance-of-payments deficit. So the 'safe' policy is to let others take the load, sit on your surplus and impose the deficits on someone else. But safe for whom, and for how long? Depression is contagious and the real question is, therefore, how can we break away from the deflationary bias that spreads the contagion and deepens unemployment in the developed world and dire poverty and death in the Third World?

The second problem is that which arises from the needs of a country like Britain, whose tradeable sector has been allowed to deteriorate to such an extent that, even in a growing world economy, the attempt to attain greater employment can be severely hampered by the excess of imports over exports. If we don't solve the problems of such countries, their stagnation will constrain the whole world economy. Unless a method is agreed of planning imports during periods of industrial reconstruction, then the weak economies will either be condemned to very slow recovery, or be forced to take unilateral action to protect their economies. That would be an international tragedy that would condemn this and future generations to greater instability and poverty.

The task before us is to avert that failure, and the 'new Bretton Woods' system is the most practical. The international co-ordination and trade planning that this implies must be based on a clearly negotiated, well understood set of rules. It cannot rely on 'pressure' or on 'market psychology'; it must provide for resources to finance trade and development and have as a main objective the promotion of manufacture, selling and employment.

In the interests of expanding production throughout the world, control of the international financial and trading system must be regained. If that does not happen the likely consequence is that the economy of the West will increasingly divide up into trading blocs engaged in trade wars, both declared and undeclared, with all of the terrible economic and political consequences. The effort to gain responsible multilateral control of the international system now enjoys widespread support in developed and developing countries. The idea that monetarist discipline offers a way to prosperity is now almost entirely confined to Mrs Thatcher and President Reagan – and he only keeps it for export. His economy is the biggest debtor in world history. The move towards implementing a different order, however, needs a lead and while this would come most quickly and authoritatively from the United States, it will not come this side of the next Presidential elections and if they see the Democrats defeated it won't come then either. Initiatives must therefore be taken by others; and particularly by the EEC. Even before the Community sets out a world agenda, it could and should in any case be pursuing a strategy for European recovery.

A STRATEGY FOR EUROPEAN RECOVERY

There are 16 million people unemployed in the 12 countries of the European Community. Six million of those people are between the ages of 15 and 25. An expansion of economic activity throughout Europe is urgent, and would of course, greatly facilitate a British recovery since the EEC countries are now our main trading partners.

Unfortunately, the main programme of economic reform now being initiated within the Community, a programme enthusiastically endorsed by Mrs Thatcher, is almost entirely irrelevant to tackling the Community's unemployment problem. Adopted at the Milan summit in 1985, the reform programme which is entitled 'Completing the Internal Market', represents a political failure of such magnitude that it may well endanger the future development and cohesion of the Community.

Many of the ideas contained in the European White Paper which outlines the programme for completing the internal market by 1992 are sensible and useful – harmonizing car exhaust emission standards at a stringent level, for example, and rationalizing plant and animal safety checks. And I support the attempt to reduce the piecemeal proliferation of non-tariff barriers to trade. This creeping protection is an inhibition to the rational development of production and trade.

But the philosophy behind the programme to complete the internal market goes far beyond these sensible technical measures. The vision is a single integrated market of 320 million people – a market greater than the internal market of the United States. The increased competition consequent upon the harmonization of fiscal systems and the removal of all physical and technical barriers to trade will, it is believed, make Europe as a whole more efficient *and* lead to an expansion of output and an expansion of prosperity *in the Community as a whole*.

This latter point is not convincing. Even the eager author of the White Paper admits, in spectacular understatement, that free movement of goods and services creates the 'risk' that prosperity will appear only in 'the areas of greatest economic advantage', and suggests that a fuller use of the Community regional funds will be necessary. But Lord Cockfield, Mrs Thatcher's choice as one of our Commissioners in Brussels, and the man responsible for the White Paper, has declared that the development of the internal market is *not* conditional on the strengthening of regional and social programmes.

All this will have a dreary familiarity for a British audience. Far from being a grand plan for European recovery, it is Thatcherism on a European scale. We have had seven years of misery in Britain and while sharing it around a little might appeal to some, the awful fact is that it would, of course, only make our condition worse.

We have learned in Britain the painful lesson that a market free-for-all is only free-for-some. Completing the internal market will no more increase employment in Europe as a whole than Mrs Thatcher's free-market economics has increased employment in Britain. It will only share relatively fewer jobs around in a different pattern, a few more jobs in Germany and

France perhaps, and a few less in Britain and Spain. That governments are only too well aware of this is indicated by the tortuous process of negotiating the harmonization, and by Mrs Thatcher's talk of open markets for financial services being in our national interest – and so, presumably, against the interests of other member states. And if that is the greatest gain she can anticipate on the swings, the industrial losses on the round-abouts would be terrible.

The policy of completing the internal market is misconceived on two counts: first, it completely fails to address the Community's major economic problem, unemployment; secondly, it fails to recognize the important differences which exist between the economies of the various members of the Community, differences which must be taken into account if any Community-wide programme is not to founder in discord.

An employment strategy for Europe is desperately needed. It should have three components:

- First, there must be co-ordinated fiscal expansion to create jobs throughout the Community.
- Secondly, there must be recognition of the different problems which individual countries face.
- Thirdly, there must be clear rules of operation, so that gains and sacrifices are fairly distributed. For example, a recent NEDO study revealed that France, Germany and Italy apply large indirect subsidies to their steel industries while British Steel not only struggles on without such aid but has adhered to output and employment reduction agreements that have been virtually ignored by the steel industries of other Common Market countries.

It is vital that the European attack on unemployment is co-ordinated. If there is no co-ordination, expanding countries will suck in imports while failing to increase their exports sufficiently to pay for them, and so their expansions will be aborted or at least retarded by balance-of-payments problems.

176

Expansionary policies will then be discredited, technological advance will falter and decline and the European economy will be even more open to commercial colonization by the producers from America and the Pacific.

That would be a shared fate, for such is the integration of economies in Europe that all failure and success is communicable to a greater or lesser degree.

The benefits of co-ordination for expansion and employment do not arise, however, solely by comparison with the disadvantages of not doing it. Those countries that expand benefit everyone else. Their increased imports create jobs in the countries from which they buy, and if expansion were co-ordinated then balance-of-payments risks would be lessened as all countries buy more from each other.

The risks would not, however, be eliminated altogether. A co-ordinated expansion will tend to benefit the stronger industrial countries at the expense of the others. So the weaker countries will find their imports growing faster than their exports – their expansion will be creating jobs abroad, not at home. This situation cannot be sustained. The expansion in the weaker countries will be cut short by balance-of-payments problems. Their slowdown will mean that they import less, so others will export less and jobs will be lost. All will suffer.

What is needed is a Community internal trade policy which ensures that, in the process of expansion, trade (and hence creation of new jobs) is distributed among all the countries in a manner which prevents the appearance of gross imbalances, in the same way in which a sensible regional policy should distribute jobs fairly within a country, discriminating in favour of the weaker regions. No country would be forced to bear an unfair burden by importing disproportionately more from the others than they buy from it. The potential for contagious deflation would be significantly reduced.

The components of this trade policy should be clearly spelt out and agreed. Variations in exchange rates will not be adequate for the task and other more direct means of adjustment will be required although any accumulation of self-defeating arbitrary barriers to trade should be vigorously resisted.

What is necessary is a rational, co-ordinated, supra-regional policy for a collection of sovereign states. If Europe were a single state, with recognized, legitimate organs of government and a single financial system organized coherently around a single lender of last resort, and that state were committed to expansionary policies and to powerful, flexible regional policies, which distributed prosperity and jobs among its component parts, then an internal trade policy would not be necessary. State discrimination between regions would do the trick. But the European Community is not of this form; nor is it likely to be. The need, therefore, is for a framework within which the benefits of a European employment programme could be attained without massive upheaval. And when such enormous amounts of time and effort are put into the complex, detailed negotiations around the issue of the internal market, I am sure that if an equivalent effort were put into an expansionary programme for Europe, into a programme of employment, then both the prospects of future prosperity and the political harmony of Europe and its peoples would be far more secure.

GETTING ON WITH IT

The Labour government will campaign actively for reforms to the international trading system and within the EEC which will provide a framework for expansion. But the condition of our country and the pressing need for change are such that our recovery programme cannot wait upon the attainment of either or both of these objectives. Realistically, we must recognize that, in the extremely difficult circumstances which we will inherit from the Tories, we will have to get on with the job without benefit of the necessary international reform. We will therefore implement our three-stage recovery programme in the context of a slow-growing world economy and a slow-growing EEC, well understanding the difficulty in both spheres.

In such circumstances we are obviously in for tough negotiations during which we commit ourselves to implementing the recovery programme as fast as is possible. We will of course use all the appropriate provisions of the EEC treaty, together with other informal means, to protect our industrial policy, taking account of the fact that other countries have and do take such safeguarding measures. And in all of that, the plain fact will remain that the recovery programme we are pursuing, especially the discriminatory measures of the industrial policy, is in the long-run interest of the Community as well as ourselves. An expanding and secure British economy is, after all, of much greater advantage to us in Britain and to our neighbours than a depressed economy dragging along in continual decline.

The external limitations on the rate at which the economy can be expanded will make our task of rebuilding British industry more difficult. But it will not deter us from that task. We are committed to the recovery of Britain's manufacturing industry because it is the key to survival. We will carry out that commitment, for the alternative is further deterioration of the standards of living and liberty of the British people.

8
Industrialization and Democratic Socialism

Throughout this book I have referred repeatedly to the seven-year record of the Thatcher government. I make no apology for doing that. It is essential that we and everyone else knows where we start from. It is vital too that every opportunity is taken of recording the consequences of having a government that preferred to accept unemployment and its monstrous costs, rather than work for employment and its obvious benefits.

That policy was not casual or hapless, it was deliberate. Unemployment and the fear of unemployment have been the essential means of imposing the discipline and the sense of deference fundamentally necessary to the fulfilment of the economic and social objectives of the so-called New Right to which Mrs Thatcher and some of her co-religionists – fewer by the day – belong.

THE NEW RIGHT

I am willing to allow that the New Right is not motivated by some devilish malice. It is just that the purposes of its convictions could simply not be achieved without a massive increase in unemployment – an increase that it has always been prepared to tolerate and ready to generate if not directly and openly advocate.

180

At its most genteel the conviction of the New Right is that private acquisitiveness is enough, in itself, to serve the public good so long as it is given its head and not constrained by social obligations like the Welfare State, or economic impediments like trade unionism, or regulations of labour protection, or, most of all, full employment. Government, it believes, should confine itself to the ancient functions of external defence and diplomacy and internal civil order, and be controlled by people and interests dedicated to limiting the state to those minimal purposes. Competition should be the great guarantee against both abuse and weakness in the market. And that market system, apart from being the strict and sensitive arbiter of commercial success, should also determine the allocation of resources to meet human needs since everything – including care and cure and opportunity – ultimately has its price, and users (the New Right holds) will only value what they buy.

It is, of course, a philosophy exhumed from the past. Seventy years ago Thorstein Veblen dismissed it as a 'system of make believe', when it was applied with greater vigour, viciousness and apparent validity than even Mrs Thatcher has achieved. Still, in our time it has been applied to devastating effect by a government elected and re-elected and it is certain that a further period of power for the 'conviction politician' would bring further doses of the morbid policies and the murderous results. Even now, the stubbornness and stridency which are otherwise regarded as evidence of inadequacy in any mature person with responsibilities are viewed as strength in the more sycophantic parts of the press, the more impressionable parts of the public and the more inert sections of the Conservative Party. In a nation that has been scolded into defeatism for years, the nasty-medicine-is-the-best-medicine, joy-through-pain politics retains an appeal.

That is 'Thatcherism' and it goes much wider in purpose and effect than the person playing the title role. If it were merely evidence of an irritating temperament in the Prime Minister it wouldn't matter much. But it does matter because it isn't mere temperament, it is awful accomplishment. For all the talk of 'freedom' it has reduced liberties of expression and choices of consumption, it has – to say the least – done nothing to combat racism or sexism, and through an epidemic increase in poverty, it has made millions more dependent upon the state. For all the talk of 'morality' it has meant the neglect of the young and the old and the sick and the ill-housed. For all the talk of 'higher standards' it has meant more ugliness and danger in the environment and coincided – I make the charitable concession – with an increase in violence (a matter of tragic fact) and vulgarity (a matter of personal taste). It has ruined lives and broken up families. It has crushed communities. And it has destroyed industries.

As we have seen, the result is that foreign importers increased their share of our home market by 40 per cent between 1979 and 1985, our share of world trade in manufactured goods went down by 23 per cent and a balance of trade *surplus* in such goods of nearly £3 billion in 1978–9 had been turned into a *deficit* of over £3 billion by 1985. Manufactured output in Britain is still 6 per cent less than it was in 1979 and the CBI forecast in September 1986 that it would be lower still by the end of the year. Manufacturing investment is still 18 per cent lower than it was in 1979 – and that is despite the temporary surge which took place before Nigel Lawson ended capital investment allowances. Unemployment is higher by two million people than in 1979 – and that is after several successful statistical efforts to beautify the figures without actually reducing the number of jobless.

On top of all that, the income from oil revenues is now declining. Mrs Thatcher's cushion is now getting thinner. Britain's great opportunity is disappearing.

Faced with that accumulated and accumulating crisis, Mrs Thatcher has retreated into a fantasy world where all of her friends are abroad, all of her enemies are within. She and her government refuse to face the crisis or combat the slump in any constructive way. Indeed, every action worsens both. Every evidence of decline seems to stiffen their resolve to repeat errors, especially the central error that Britain's multiple economic, industrial and social problems can somehow be eased by scattering tax cut confetti over them.

THE CONSTRUCTIVE ALTERNATIVE

To deal with that crisis we need not only an Alternative Economic Strategy but also a political strategy for an Alternative Economy and Society. It is on such a strategy that my colleagues and I promoted public discussion and debate with our campaigns for Jobs and Industry, and presented our proposals as the Party of Production. It is a strategy based on investment in change and on harnessing new technologies for recovery and for re-distribution. It is a strategy for development and for correcting the present imbalance between big and small business, between the selfish and the social institutions of our economy and between those who get their living by earning and those who get it by owning.

It is a strategy based on agreement rather than disagreement; for industrial democracy and co-operation rather than conflict and confrontation. It means new forms of planning to change the major options for our economy and society; planning *for and by agreement* through negotiation of change and extension of collective bargaining; planning through democracy and for democratization, rather than the clumsy cruelty of the centralized commissar state or the chaotic privatized market of the Thatcher economy. It means planning for recovery in the local and regional economy, for a national shift of savings into investment through agencies such as the British Investment Bank. It means both taking the risk and spreading the risk of investing in our own and our children's futures. And it also means an international strategy for co-operation to promote recovery in the European and the global economies.

None of that is soft or easy or cheap. None of it is all give and no take. Nothing worth having is or can be. Indeed, there is only one soft option for government. It is throwing in the towel, letting everyone else take the pain and the blame like this Tory government does. And there is only one thing more expensive than meeting the challenges and the costs of the changes that are vital to our survival, and that is *not* meeting those demands. The result of the failure to invest in people and machines is seen in the horrific bills of idleness and decay. There is no bargain there. The result of the failure to plan is guaranteed defeat, for it means being caught by surprise so that we are outflanked by every new change, overwhelmed by every new demand.

'Plan' is a nasty four-letter word for the present Prime Minister, yet every company that deserves the chance of survival makes plans. Every household plans, however informally, its broad relation between income and expenditure. Our leading competitors plan, though they may hide behind a screen of non-intervention. The Japanese plan, the South Koreans plan. And they plan ahead, looking five, ten or fifteen years into the future, assessing and accounting for tomorrow's techniques and technologies rather than seeking a low-wage, low-tech economy.

What we need in government, in unions, and in business itself is *workshops* rather than *talkshops* if we are to match the challenge of new technologies and reverse our industrial decline with a decade of reconstruction and regeneration of British industry. To those who claim that planning by agreement does not go far enough I stress that our planning has to be to a great extent *with* the market rather than against the market. But it is very deliberately for change through widened economic and industrial democracy, with social accountability and control, making it possible to harness the resources, skills and energies of both the big and small battalions of British business in the campaign for more jobs with lower costs and better rewards. I believe that planning by agreement is the most natural and necessary extension of collective bargaining and not a reversal or an alternative to it in any way.

I heeded a long time ago the words of R. H. Tawney that it is essential for modern government and modern people to ensure 'the development of machinery to secure that the larger questions of economic strategy and industrial organisation are treated as what in fact they are, *a public concern* [my italics], and that those who decide them must be accountable to the public for the tenor of their decisions'. That is not the corporate state. Indeed it is the very opposite, for it means a structure for deliberation and decision-making which must relate directly to the people of the country and not rule over them.

Against the background of the ruinous record of the Thatcher government in manufacturing investment there is not only scope, but a patent need, to defend public involvement in the British economy. The need to defend social ownership of national assets is imperative. The government has raised £15,000 million so far through changing ownership rather than increasing investment and in the process has enabled massive speculative gains by under-pricing our national assets. In Amersham International investors have seen their shares increase by double against the *Financial Times* All-Share Index, 50 per cent more in the sale of Associated British Ports. Shares in British Telecom are well above the comparable increase in the FT index, while Jaguar shares have quadrupled over the FT index. Never in the history of modern economic management has so much been offered for so little to so few.

The reason, of course, is clear. The Tory Party by such sales is not only serving the interests of its own subscribers and friends but it is trying to offset the disastrous decline in revenues which comes from the loss of industries, jobs and incomes. Without such sales and without North Sea oil revenues its own client class in finance and in the City would have already turned its wrath against the government itself.

Indeed, disillusionment and demand for change are now clearly apparent among those who once gave a constituency to Mrs Thatcher's reactionary radicalism. The concerned CBI, the anxious Chambers of Commerce, the working managers who scorn the idea that privatization and tax sharings can meet industrial needs, the young professionals in business and trade and technology who know that planning and intervention and investment support are practical necessities, now realize increasingly that what they believed to be a direction from a government of 'enterprise' has turned out to be a dogma from a government of wandering ideologues. They, like the rest of Britain, now look for a commitment to industrial regeneration by planned expansion as an essential foundation of resilient recovery and improved competitiveness. And they know that in the process British government must be at least as ready to intervene and to deliberately sponsor growth, to play to strengths and to assist in the development of trade and technology as the governments of competitor countries.

They and the country in general will have that commitment and the action that goes with it from the next Labour government. To *extend* public involvement we do not offer state business run by bureaucrats, we do not say 'Whitehall knows best' and we certainly do not favour the economic incest between big business and the State which passes for policy in the Social Democratic Party. Our policies are for a plural public sector extending the forms of ownership and control within the framework of a new industrial democracy. That means:

- We are committed to social ownership of sectors of activity where there are natural or technical monopolies which best serve the public interest through an overall national agency.
- We are committed to a British Investment Bank, not as an agency for channelling all national savings but as a means for ensuring that a necessary share of resources of financial institutions are channelled into investment in this country rather than siphoned off into investments in property, finance or industry abroad.
- We are committed to introducing British Enterprise as a public holding company taking shares in enterprises in return for the injection of public funds.

- We are committed to increasing and strengthening regional, metropolitan and local enterprise boards and agencies.
- We are committed to major support for co-operative enterprise, not only in distribution but also in industry and services. Such enterprise has flourished especially in European countries such as France and Spain and provided opportunities where other systems of ownership fear to tread.

Such a mixture and diversity of forms of ownership and control are vital if we are to add the economic enfranchisement of working people to the political franchise.

In short, the genuine mixed and plural economy is *ours* as democratic socialists; not theirs as public sector destroyers and private sector shrinkers. The Thatcher government presides over a dual economy divided between finance and industry and unequal competition between big and small business. It results in increasing concentration of economic power, decreasing opportunities for employment and a future in which a small, opulent, money-handling class co-exists with a shanty economy that is occasionally relieved by a warehouse or assembly plant.

INDUSTRIALIZATION AND SOCIAL PROGRESS

That is not a future that can be tolerated. That is why in practice and in principle we must apply the productionist view which I have put forward in this book. It is not merely or even mainly a philosophy of industrialization. It is a conviction about social progress. Without a sustained and sustainable improvement in the material strength of our economy and the material conditions of life, social progress – whether measured as educational opportunity or decent pensions, cultural standards or personal liberty, freedom from the fear of illness or freedom from the menace of violence – democratic confidence and vitality will stumble and fall. Such emancipation is not merely a by-product of economic sufficiency, it is dependent upon it. High though the ideals and strong though the connections of toleration and liberty may be, they are nevertheless capable of being choked by prolonged insecurity and the conflicts which it inevitably provokes.

Insecurity imposes its own tyranny and produces its own despots and serfs. Socialism came into being to overwhelm that insecurity. Democratic socialism developed when it became necessary to establish to supporters, opponents and doubters that the means chosen to defeat the tyranny was the collective, deliberative and democratic power of parliaments – and that meant the system and the method and not just the places. I am a democratic socialist because I believe that a commitment to the freedom and dignity of the individual, to the construction of a society which is compassionate and fair, in which people are judged on their merit and are enabled to develop their abilities to the full, requires the control of the forces of production, distribution, exchange and communication by that society through a variety of democratic means. The belief started as an instinct; it was moulded into a political conviction by the knowledge that an economy that was not subject to democracy was an open season for the few who were already strong and powerful, or the few who could get to be so by exploitation, and a democracy not subject to the requirements of efficient production and fair distribution was little more than a pleasant adornment. I wasn't very bothered and I am still not very bothered by titles. 'What matters,' said R. H. Tawney 'is the facts, not the names by which they are called. The important question is not whether an undertaking is described as private or public – it is whether, if it is private, adequate guarantees can be established that it performs a public function, and whether, if it is public, it performs it effectively.' The 'public function' is in my view to fulfil the goals of freedom, fairness and opportunity, which necessarily requires fulfilling the goals of production efficiently in terms of the cost of resources, the treatment of the environment and the value to those who need to consume the product.

Although capitalism has undoubtedly fostered the major

growth in material wealth which has distinguished the past 200 years from what went before, it has frequently done that by dividing society, by limiting freedom and limiting opportunity. And often it has done that by imposing enormous costs on those least able to bear them. Moreover, the institutions of free-market capitalism have been shown to be incapable of sustaining the employment and accumulation which is supposed to be the superior quality and the justification of the unequal system. The experiences of the thirties, and of war-time planning and co-operation, both in the domestic economy and in the international economy, produced the realization that there was a better way, and a determination not to return to the follies and cruelties of pre-war economic policy. Managing the market – the international market and the home market – was not only desirable but possible.

Unfortunately, the vision and commitment which characterized the early post-war years were not sustained. The institutions and procedures created in those early years laid the foundations for 25 years of remarkable prosperity throughout the West, but they were not developed and adapted. The new approach to the economy was not pushed forward, gaining more and more social control over the vagaries and inequities of the market. Instead, the progress came to a halt. Indeed, the gains that had been made were slowly, but surely, eroded.

The failure of ideas and institutions to keep up with a changing world meant that, inevitably, those institutions would crack under the strain of the new problems, the new challenges, which 40 years have brought. No-one, however, could have predicted that the consequence would be not a renewal of progress, but a slide *backwards*, a dismantling of much of what had been achieved and a return to the failed ideas of the thirties. The lurch backwards in economic thinking and in economic policy has brought great instability to the Western world, and contributed to the slow-down in the growth of the West, the rise in unemployment to pre-war levels, debt, poverty and famine in under-developed countries and the failure – in some cases the deliberate evasion – by Western governments in their duty of devising and implementing coherent strategies for tackling these problems.

Of the advanced countries, it is Britain that has suffered most from the economic nihilism of the Right. The policies of Mrs Thatcher's governments have not only divided and embittered Britain, they have impoverished Britain. At the same time as they have created great need, they have diminished the capacity of the British economy to satisfy need. Their profligacy has ensured that even with significant change the next ten years will be difficult years, even hard years, for the British people. Without such change further decline will be steep, miserable and inevitable.

COMMON SENSE

In this situation of economic emergency the values of democratic socialism assume an even greater importance. For not only does democratic socialism have the vision to define the direction in which we must move out of this mess, but also, it is by its very nature a practical and common-sense creed.

'Common sense' is a term which some socialists do not find attractive. They scorn it as an alibi for giving up on social and economic progress because the battles to be fought are too tough, and for disguising loss of nerve and will. To characterize common sense as a retreat is not only a distortion of the language, but also betrays a dangerously cavalier attitude to the real lives of real people. Common sense is not a loss of political will, it is the assertion of strong political commitment to the pursuit of realistic, attainable goals which can and will be met. Most important of all, common sense means caring for people, for people's jobs, their homes, their health, their children's education, their parents' comfortable retirement. Democratic socialists have a high regard for common sense because they pursue their goals and attempt to push society in the direction they want it to go *democratically*, that is by persuasion, by organization, by political means, listening to people and working with them to attain the goals that we believe to be right. And common sense means refusing to endanger the livelihoods of those whom we wish to serve by foolhardy gestures made romantically and, in my view, selfishly to prove purist credentials.

The romantics and the purists are not, of course, the only critics of common sense. There are others who, over the past few years, have suggested that the democratic socialism for which the Labour Party has always stood – the 'common sense' approach – is 'outmoded', that the 'sociological' base of the Labour Party's support has been withered away by the decline of the great urban industrial conurbations, by the falling proportion of blue-collar workers in the labour force, and by the rapid growth of mortgage-holding, car-owning, suburban white-collar workers. The typical supporter of the Labour Party is portrayed as a man in a cloth cap and a boiler suit.

This image of the Labour supporter is profoundly inaccurate. But, more important than the inaccuracy of the caricature is the failure to understand the nature of democratic socialism as a growing political philosophy which is just as relevant to the problems of society today as it was to the society of the late nineteenth century, or the thirties, or the era of post-war reconstruction – all periods in which the values and the actions of democratic socialism served this country well.

In a world in which economic change is more rapid than ever before, the costs of change, too, are greater than ever before. New technological developments render old skills and old factories redundant with frightening speed. Yet to try to prevent that change would endanger the economic future of the whole country. Moreover, the full exploitation of the advantages of modern technology require organization on a greater scale than was previously the case. This in turn implies that the impact of technological change is more widespread, so that no job, no enterprise is untouched.

Economic change and increasing affluence have brought with

them a greater fragmentation of our society. The decline of the extended family and the support systems which characterized working-class communities has become a sociological cliché. This does not mean it is untrue, or that the pressures associated with that disappearance are not real. But nor does it mean that a socialist movement should wallow in nostalgia for the old days of terraced housing, minimal health care and few educational opportunities. Only those who never knew it could really long for it. Socialism is dedicated to progress. And progress means using the fruits of science and technology, of accumulation and production to enhance the living standards and the opportunities of all the people. But in the process social strains do emerge. People have become more isolated, more vulnerable.

Economic growth has also imposed a far greater commercial pressure upon society than was previously the case. In consumption, in the arts and entertainment, in sports, in newspapers, in the battering of the environment, in every aspect of daily life the pressure of financial calculation and exploitation has increased and is increasing. Of course, commercial pressure can break down old semi-feudal systems of exploitation, open up opportunity and give enormous pleasure. But clearly commercialism is often crass and destructive. The ability of techological change to liberate and enhance peoples' lives can be all too often suffocated by the oppressive effects of commercial exploitation.

Social control of the market is necessary if we are to reap the advantages of accumulation and modern technology, and not be used by them. Only social control of the market can mitigate and mediate in those commercial pressures which, if left unchecked, debase our lives. Only social control of the market can provide the collective answer to the alienation and isolation which can accompany material progress. Most important of all, only social control of the market can, at one and the same time, ensure a fair distribution of the costs and benefits of change, and maintain the efficient operation of that highly complex, interdependent system, the modern economy. And this is as true of the international financial and trading system as it is of the domestic economy.

192

To achieve these goals social control of the market must mean democratic control. Not just to make it acceptable; but to make it efficient. For not only is the market incapable of maintaining full employment and efficient accumulation (as has been amply demonstrated in recent years), but also the market must be subject to democratic control if we are to use the ideas and talents of all the people and prevent – under any system of ownership – the selfish senility that can overtake power.

The divisive policies of the Thatcher governments have wasted many talents by cramping and limiting opportunities. Concerted action will be necessary to rebuild and modernize our economy, and that concerted action will involve not only the re-organization of production, but also the re-organization of employment, education and training, research and design. Particular efforts are necessary to stop the neglect of abilities and rights and the prevention of full freedom of achievement that has afflicted and still afflicts women, black people, the disabled and all those, in majority and in minority, who have not fitted the convenience of a society run by and for established classes of class, sex and skin colour. The failure to provide such fair treatment and fair chances has in some ways been inadvertent, a product of convention rather than conspiracy. In other cases it has come from prejudice and deliberate oppression. The causes are important only in so far as they show unconscious or conscious offence against fellow human beings. The results are the same and it will take deliberate action to change the condition and achieve justice and efficiency.

The belief in common sense and merit; the commitment to the female majority and the black minority; the concern with management; the objective of enhancing the negotiating strength and influence of trade unionism; the acceptance of plurality in ownership; the commitment to cleansing the environment; the determination to emphasize and exploit technology; all this – together with much else – will be regarded as evidence of deviation by a small number of socialists who have a rigid view of ownership, of class, of expectations and relationships that is not, in my opinion, recognizable as reality. In some cases their attitude, again in my constant view, is the result of a narrowness of perception reminiscent of theocrats. In others it seems to come from shallowness of conviction; they seem to lack the confidence that democratic socialism is a creed and a commitment which draws life from realities and is not threatened or defiled by being matched to social and economic change.

The common sense of this is in some quarters – or, more accurately, some smaller fractions – regarded as being an attempt to magnetize the 'upwardly mobile'. Political opponents condemn it as being a 'smiling face of socialism disguising the real expropriating and authoritarian thing'. I expect such demonology. It is the stock-in-trade of the cynical, the superstitious and the political child-frighteners among our critics. It fits in with red scares, the 'Labour will introduce the Gestapo' claim of 1945, and its later variations.

In our own ranks, however, the complaints are just as excitable and mistaken. There is a criticism that an 'upwardly mobile' appeal has no place in the armoury of socialism. That is profoundly wrong and defeatist, for my view – and one that I share with socialists across the world – is that our beliefs exist to promote upward mobility of whole countries and, by definition, the individuals within those countries. The ambition stems partly from the belief in amelioration and emancipation. But it comes too from the knowledge that if we are not directly engaged in the upward economic, social and political mobility of people, they face a fate of downward mobility or, at best, stagnation.

We do not believe, of course, that upward mobility can or should depend *solely* on individual effort or the ability of the specific individual to make it, regardless of class, race, sex or social and economic background. While we welcome personal effort, hard work and achievement, and believe that these should be acknowledged and rewarded, we also know that a whole society and large groups in that society cannot be lifted, given upward mobility, without collective provision and collective effort. We believe, therefore, not only in the upward mobility of individuals (like many of us who are socialists) who have the energy, or youth, or inventiveness, or opportunity, or luck, or the support of families and the community, or whatever else it takes to be upwardly mobile. We believe in the 'upward mobility' of, for example, children and young people, who would otherwise know only drudgery, the sick who otherwise would be stuck with their pain and disability, pensioners who would otherwise endure poverty and loneliness. We consider, in short, that the privilege of strength is the power which it gives to help those who are not strong out of their weakness – to make them 'upwardly mobile'. And if and when that power buckles, or better still, destroys class boundaries of snobbery and privilege – and inverted snobbery and under-privilege – that is an unreserved victory of belief and of practical provision.

It is this which is the real test, not just because everything must be precisely justified on grounds of prosaic practicality – that would be arid and limiting – but because we as socialists want to be judged by deeds of production and provision. In all of that we bear in mind and in practice Bevan's maxim that 'at least two considerations' should determine the course of policy and action: 'its applicability to the immediate situation certainly, but also its faithfulness to the general body of principles which make up your philosophy. Without the latter, politics is merely a job like any other.'

MAKING OUR WAY

The objective and the means are audacious. Faced with the inherited condition and the extent of need, the path towards the industrial, economic and social recovery which is a matter of survival for our country and essential to the future of ourselves and our children is very tough. But we will tread it with determination and, because the course is so necessary, we will keep on pursuing it. The alternatives are misery for Britain and powerless opposition for our Movement. That is why I believe that it is better to get on with the job than to be paralysed by the size of it. Better to work for decisive victories of socialism than wait for some interminable date when they can be universal. Better to light a candle, than curse the darkness.

Index

Index